Thinkers for Architects

Architects have often looked to philosophers and theorists from beyond the discipline for design inspiration or in search of a critical framework for practice. This original series offers quick, clear introductions to key thinkers who have written about architecture and whose work can yield insights for designers.

> 'Each unintimidatingly slim book makes sense of the subjects' complex theories.'
>
> Building Design

> '...a valuable addition to any studio space or computer lab'
>
> Architectural Record

> '...a creditable attempt to present their subjects in a useful way'
>
> Architectural Review

Deleuze and Guattari for Architects
Andrew Ballantyne

Heidegger for Architects
Adam Sharr

Irigaray for Architects
Peg Rawes

Bhabha for Architects
Felipe Hernández

Bourdieu for Architects
Helena Webster

Benjamin for Architects

Brian Elliott

Derrida for Architects

Richard Coyne

Merleau-Ponty for Architects

Jonathan Hale

Derrida

for

Architects

Richard Coyne

Routledge
Taylor & Francis Group

LONDON AND NEW YORK

First published 2011
by Routledge
2 Park Square, Milton Park, Abingdon, Oxon OX14 4RN

Simultaneously published in the USA and Canada
by Routledge
711 Third Avenue, New York, NY 10017

Routledge is an imprint of the Taylor & Francis Group, an informa business

British Library Cataloguing in Publication Data
A catalogue record for this book is available from the British Library

Library of Congress Cataloging-in-Publication Data
Derrida for architects / Richard Coyne.
p. cm. – (Thinkers for architects ; 7)
Includes bibliographical references and index.
1. Derrida, Jacques. 2. Architecture–Philosophy. I. Title.
B2430.D484C69 2011
194–dc22
2010046626

ISBN: 978-0-415-59178-2 (hbk)
ISBN: 978-0-415-59179-9 (pbk)
ISBN: 978-0-203-81662-2 (ebk)

Typeset in Frutiger and Galliard
by Wearset Ltd, Boldon, Tyne and Wear

Printed and bound in Great Britain by
TJ International Ltd, Padstow, Cornwall

To Philip

Contents

Acknowledgements   xi

Series Editor's Preface   xii

Prologue   xiv

1 Thinking about Architecture   1

Juxtapositions and oppositions 2

Totalising strategies 4

Agonistics 5

Confounding oppositions 7

2 Language and Architecture   8

Language and history 11

Correspondence 13

Sign systems and difference 16

Deep structure 19

Widening the scope of language 20

Radicalising Structuralism 22

Meaning and metaphysics 23

3 Intertextuality and Metaphor   25

Writing as a drug 28

Proto-writing 31

Implications for architecture 33

4 Derrida on Architecture   36

Chora L Works 47

5   Other Spaces   61

    Crossing the line 67
    Space and paradox 71

6   Derrida and Radical Practice   74

    Interpretation 78
    Radical hermeneutics 81
    Institutions 83
    Activism and the radicalisation of architectural practices 86
    Radical pedagogy 91
    Radical media 93

    Notes for Further Reading   99
    References   101
    Index   112

Acknowledgements

I would like to acknowledge the assistance of numerous colleagues in the School of Arts, Culture and Environment at the University of Edinburgh in helping develop these themes and for providing feedback. I would like to thank Anastasia Karandinou for her guidance on clarity, and Adam Sharr, series editor, for his helpful advice. As ever I acknowledge the inspiration of Adrian Snodgrass in introducing me to the themes of Deconstruction and hermeneutics.

Image credit

Series Editor's Preface

Adam Sharr

Architects have often looked to thinkers in philosophy and theory for design ideas, or in search of a critical framework for practice. Yet architects and students of architecture can struggle to navigate thinkers' writings. It can be daunting to approach original texts with little appreciation of their contexts. And existing introductions seldom explore architectural material in any detail. This original series offers clear, quick and accurate introductions to key thinkers who have written about architecture. Each book summarises what a thinker has to offer for architects. It locates their architectural thinking in the body of their work, introduces significant books and essays, helps decode terms and provides quick reference for further reading. If you find philosophical and theoretical writing about architecture difficult, or just don't know where to begin, this series will be indispensable.

Books in the *Thinkers for Architects* series come out of architecture. They pursue architectural modes of understanding, aiming to introduce a thinker to an architectural audience. Each thinker has a unique and distinctive ethos, and the structure of each book derives from the character at its focus. The thinkers explored are prodigious writers and any short introduction can only address a fraction of their work. Each author – an architect or an architectural critic – has focused on a selection of a thinker's writings which they judge most relevant to designers and interpreters of architecture. Inevitably, much will be left out. These books will be the first point of reference, rather than the last word, about a particular thinker for architects. It is hoped that they will encourage you to read further; offering an incentive to delve deeper into the original writings of a particular thinker.

The *Thinkers for Architects* series has proved highly successful, expanding now to eight volumes dealing with familiar cultural figures whose writings have influenced architectural designers, critics and commentators in distinctive and important ways. Books explore the work of: Gilles Deleuze and Felix Guattari, Martin Heidegger, Luce Irigaray, Homi Bhabha, Pierre Bourdieu and Maurice Merleau-Ponty. The series continues to expand, addressing an increasingly rich diversity of contemporary thinkers who have something to say to architects.

Adam Sharr is Professor of Architecture at the University of Newcastle-upon-Tyne, Principal of Adam Sharr Architects and Editor (with Richard Weston) of *arq: Architectural Research Quarterly*, Cambridge University Press' international architecture journal. His books include *Heidegger for Architects*.

Prologue

Jacques Derrida (1930–2004) was among the few philosophers who wrote explicitly about architecture and engaged with architects. He was born in the French colony of Algeria into a Jewish family. He studied philosophy at the École Normale Supérieure in Paris, where he spent most of his academic career, though he travelled extensively and was closely connected with several universities in the USA. Derrida's recent biography by David Mikics presents Derrida as a highly controversial figure (Mikics, 2010, pp. 69–70). In spite of the respect he was accorded abroad, Derrida did not fit comfortably within the academic system in Paris. He did not receive his doctorate until 1980, which was based on works previously published (Powell, 2006, p. 40). Derrida's most important writings appeared in the 1960s, with his engagement by architects flourishing 20 years later in the mid-1980s.

My main point in this book is to renew an interest in the thinking of Jacques Derrida for architects. Derrida's ideas were carried over into architecture as justification for the emergence of a new style, the architecture of 'Deconstruction' in the 1980s and 1990s. I contend that this movement (Deconstruction) falls short of realising what is radical in Derrida's contribution to understanding architecture. So I will re-evaluate Derrida's contribution and argue for the further development of its potential. I emphasize Derrida's contribution to the way architecture is practised, thought about and taught, rather than the forms and spaces produced by Deconstructive architecture. Through this analysis Derrida has two main contributions to make. First is a new understanding of the *institution* of architecture opened up by his arguments, that is, architecture as an authoritative profession with accreditation, organisation, standards, leadership, archives and a 'canon' (examples of fine buildings). Second are the intellectual procedures by which Derrida goes about his analyses of texts and his resolution of philosophical problems. His *approaches* are as useful for architecture as are the philosophical conclusions that he reaches.

I contend that this movement (Deconstruction) falls short of realising what is radical in Derrida's contribution to understanding architecture.

This prologue begins with a brief overview of the main themes in Derrida's writing. Chapter 1 will develop his thinking from an architectural perspective, in particular the strategy of thinking in terms of oppositions. In architecture we may think of oppositions between inside and outside, front and back, public and private, structure and ornament. Derrida deals more directly with oppositions such as speaking and writing, signifiers and signifieds, centres and margins. Chapter 2 deals in more detail with Derrida's contribution to architecture via his understanding of language: how it operates and what are its problems. Chapter 3 presents the theme of language as a matter of how we write things down, the role of text. It is common enough to think of architecture as a text or a form of writing. Derrida introduces strategies of writing that make much of the interlinking of textural references. I argue that here Derrida's writing has greatest resonance with ideas about design, as motivated, inspired and propelled through a constellation of rich associations. In Chapter 4 I examine Derrida's encounter with architects in some detail, and in Chapter 5 the implications of his thoughts on space. Chapter 6 places Derrida in the intellectual landscape and seeks to explain what is radical about his thinking for architects.

In writing about Derrida the temptation is to attempt to write as Derrida might write, to deploy linguistic colour, indirect allusions, assume ready access to a rich body of intellectual material and to really make the reader work hard. Any such effect on the reader of this book could be only accidental. I try to explain, illuminate, and clarify Derrida's thinking. The danger of any such simplification is that we short-change Derrida, rendering the complexity of this thought banal and easy to digest and categorise. I can only hope this book will prompt the reader to read and understand Derrida further.

Foundations

As a starting point it is worth thinking about Derrida's philosophy in terms of his objections to certainties or foundations in intellectual and cultural life. Architectural discourse readily drifts into an appeal to absolutes, not least in architecture's deployment of terms such as 'essence'. An essence is the supposedly true nature of a thing; what you are left with when you strip away its inessential or accidental properties. The essence is an unchanging core on which every other property depends, an absolute of sorts. So a design architect may try to grasp the *essential* character of wood, stone and glass, seek the essence of a site (its *genius loci*), the core and defining character of a city or landscape, to which everyone may subscribe and that will assert itself, once explained, as its incontrovertible character. In so far as a critic or consumer of architecture might appeal to the true meaning of Chartres Cathedral, the essence of Palladio's Villa Rotunda, the core values of architecture, or the essential user, they are giving expression to an irresistible appeal to foundations and certainties as the final arbiter when making a judgement. For example, in validating his approach to a 'pattern language' for architecture, Christopher Alexander appeals to several foundational precepts:

> **This is a fundamental view of the world. It says that when you build a thing you cannot merely build that thing in isolation, but must also repair the world around it, and within it, so that the larger world at that one place becomes more coherent, and more whole; and the thing which you make takes its place in the web of nature, as you make it.**
>
> (Alexander *et al.*, 1977, p. xiii)

Such appeals to coherence, wholeness, completeness and subservience to nature are appropriate illustrations of what we might call the *metaphysical* in architecture, evident also in more recent thinking about intricately folded architectural forms made possible through computer-aided design and manufacture: 'the fusion of disparate elements into continuity, the becoming whole of components that retain their status as pieces in a larger composition' (Lynn, 2004, p. 9). Derrida targets such appeals to coherent unities, as absolutes, foundations and metaphysical.

In an essay about architecture, Derrida focuses specifically on the primary importance accorded in the architectural tradition to concepts of home, dwelling and hearth, the nostalgia within modern architecture for an origin, a set of primary principles, an ordering, including deference to the sacred origins of architecture. He also notes how architecture aims for social betterment and the service of humankind, as well as the pursuit of beauty, harmony and completeness. For Derrida these pursuits are reinforced by architecture's investment in tangible permanent structure, which conspires to render 'architecture as the last fortress of metaphysics' (Derrida, 1986, p. 328).

Derrida's targeting of foundationalism in architecture is but a minor target in his project against *metaphysics*. Metaphysics refers to supposed principles and foundations that underpin any discipline, including scientific observation and rationality. So Derrida's philosophy is sceptical about foundations, absolutes and certainties to knowledge, be they the laws of nature, moral principles, standards of beauty, ideals, transcendence, or even common sense.

Derrida's philosophy is sceptical about foundations, absolutes and certainties to knowledge, be they the laws of nature, moral principles, standards of beauty, ideals, transcendence, or even common sense.

Derrida's scepticism towards absolutes is a useful starting point, to be elaborated in the rest of this book. It is not so difficult in an age of rampant relativism to show the problems with absolutist assertions and we do not need help from Derrida in identifying the problem with certainties. Declarations of supposedly unquestionable moral principles invariably invite dispute and are commonly characterised as 'undecidable', or at least subject to exceptions, caveats and the vagaries of social change. As well as the uncertainties that surround the humanities (history, cultural theory, philosophy, politics), even supposedly immutable scientific principles are subject to refinement, evolution and debate. The peculiarities of quantum physics for some provides evidence that uncertainty resides within the fabric of nature, as developed in Werner Heisenberg's so-called 'uncertainty principle' (Heisenberg, 1958). On the other hand, life without absolutes is often thought to be beyond rational study, ungrounded and meaningless. According to the philosopher Richard Bernstein, ardent *relativism* accompanies *absolutism* as an unresolved and anxious substrate to intellectual and cultural life (Bernstein, 1983).

The critique of metaphysics has been a staple for intellectuals in the twentieth century. Derrida's contribution is to analyse assertions made even by metaphysics' most strident critics and show that the critics are themselves operating metaphysically. So, political anarchists denigrate the rule of law but inevitably appeal to submission to some rule or meta-rule; atheists have their substitutes for a totalising god concept; liberal educators impose constraints among their acolytes; and relativists assert the absolute truth that all truths are relative. Derrida is less interested in the contradictions displayed by such soft targets, but prefers to tackle the heavyweight Phenomenologists, Structuralists and literary doyens of European intellectual life who claim as their radical project the complete dismantling of metaphysical thinking.

Scholars who read Derrida see his project as instructive not only in dismantling metaphysics, but appreciate and learn from the processes by which he arrives at these conclusions. Derrida's arguments towards the dismantling of certainties leave in their wake a host of new vocabularies, terms, approaches to reading and writing and methods of achieving understanding. The philosopher John Caputo claims a new kind of intellectual freedom through Derrida's strategies (Caputo, 1987, p. 209). By this reading, scholars and critics ought to rely less on the external verification of supposed certainties when putting forward their arguments and attend instead to the real business of discussion: saying what they think, disclosing presuppositions, declaring doubts and doing so in actual situations rather than in the abstract. Derrida's arguments against metaphysics are also arguments in favour of addressing particularities rather than generalities.

Here we encounter one of the many difficulties readers have in understanding Derrida. Derrida does not propose the complete abandonment of certainties, foundations, essences and the concept of a core to knowledge, a centre to our understanding. After all 'the notion of a structure lacking any center represents the unthinkable itself' (Derrida, 1966, p. 278). I'll elaborate on such apparent contradictions in Derrida's thinking in the rest of this book.

Derrida's style

Apart from his tussle with metaphysics, one of the strengths, and impediments, to reading Derrida is his mode of delivery, his style of writing, which has been described as polemical, heroic, magisterial and admitting of no self-doubt, even on this issue of uncertainty. At times he seems simply to take a view opposed to that which prevails among his intellectual peers. Mikics describes Derrida as a 'contrarian to the end' (Mikics, 2010, p. 213). Derrida might draw respectfully on the insights of others, but rarely proffers simple agreement. His writing contains no helpful literature reviews to set the intellectual context of an argument. There is no comparing and contrasting of rival authors' positions. Derrida seems always to write as though something vital is at stake intellectually, or he needs to correct an errant standpoint in his opponent. Derrida does not take a back seat to a higher authority. His introduction to the philosopher Edmund Husserl's (1859–1938) essay 'Origin of Geometry' is longer than the essay, and stresses the way Husserl himself in fact betrays his own position (Derrida, 1989a), that there can ever be an origin, for example. Derrida could not write as others write on Derrida, sublimating their own position and seeking to explain another.

Derrida's writing is also 'grammatological', in the sense that it deals in scripts and the way words are presented, with copious footnotes, italicised words from the Greek and many of the conventions of typography, arguably highly attractive to bibliophiles, but an obstacle to non-academics. Consider the following quotation as an introduction to Derrida's thinking about metaphysics in an article called 'Différance':

> ...it can be called the play of the trace. The play of a trace which no longer belongs to the horizon of Being, but whose play transports and encloses the meaning of Being: the play of the trace, or the *différance*, which has no meaning and is not. Which does not belong. There is no maintaining, and no depth to, this bottomless chessboard on which Being is put into play.
>
> (Derrida, 1982a, p. 22)

In subsequent chapters I will present other extracts from Derrida's writing that are more prosaic. In fact the interviews and seminar extracts now available for all on YouTube and other online media reveal a transparency in Derrida's speaking at variance with his use of the written word. But what can we make of this extract? Admittedly the sentences are here displaced from their context, but the sentence construction and irregular use of grammar demonstrated here can make reading Derrida difficult in any case. One of Derrida's translators, Barbara Johnson, describes Derrida's writing as often 'unspeakable', with grammar and sentence construction that militates against the possibility of it being read out loud. Derrida makes allusions to the writing of different scholars in the same paragraph, sometimes assuming recognition by the reader. His essays seem to begin as if midway in a conversation and fade out at the end as if so much more is left to be said. As well as cunning word play and overt punning, there is the deliberate denial of the logical principle of the 'excluded middle', that two opposing concepts can in fact both be the case (Johnson, 1981, pp. xvi–xvii). At times Derrida seems to assert that an entity can be both all black and all white, either or neither, and/or undecidable.

At times Derrida seems to assert that an entity can be both all black and all white, either or neither, and/or undecidable.

The extract from 'Différance', quoted above, foregrounds the word 'Being', which starts with a capital letter. The extract is about Being, the supposedly immutable, unchanging, foundational essence of being human, given a critical and sceptical treatment by the philosopher Martin Heidegger (1889–1976). The use of this word highlights a further difficulty in reading Derrida. He offers few concessions to the non-philosophically trained reader, and the reader untrained in a particular body of philosophical and literary work, in this case Phenomenology. Derrida cannot easily be read by most of us in isolation, without the company of translators' notes and commentaries explaining the background and context of his arguments. So Derrida now comes to us as a discourse, with a multitude of translators, interpreters, critics and authors, rather than as singular works from a particular author.

So Derrida now comes to us as a discourse, with a multitude of translators, interpreters, critics and authors, rather than as singular works from a particular author.

The excerpt includes the word *'différance'*, a word in French apparently invented by Derrida. It combines 'difference' and 'defer', the latter implying 'delay'. Derrida affirms, through many examples, that the extent to which human experience and intellectual life is underpinned by anything at all, the supporting structure is neither certainty nor uncertainty, but the differences between things. Difference here stands in place of the metaphysical quest for foundations. Derrida is following an argument advanced by Heidegger. But *différance* here implies a delayed existence, something that is on hold, that leaves behind itself a trail or memory. The idea of the 'play of the trace' suggests a remaindered, incidental remnant, something erased, the traces of which mingle with other remnants. Derrida's metaphor of the chessboard is accompanied by a strange qualification that it is 'bottomless', as well as having no depth. There is a suggestion that any pretence at certainty is but a play on a chessboard that has no base. The board extends down to infinity. Perhaps the search for meaning, or even the particular meaning of a statement in language, is like playing on the edge or hovering over an abyss or a chasm.

Hopefully, by the end of this book both I and the reader will be better placed to understand this extract, including what Derrida means by difference, *différance*, Being, trace, play, abyss, meaning and more besides, and how they relate to architecture. So I am asking the reader to delay understanding. The necessity of this delay is a feature of understanding in any case, according to Derrida. Understanding is always on hold, delayed, provisional, waiting for something else to come along. Twenty years after the essay in which this extract appeared, Derrida also had something to say about another word in the extract, 'maintaining', or 'maintenance', in the context of architecture. Used with deliberate irony, *maintenant* is the French word for 'now'. The now, the present, is subject to delays.

There is no single way to read Derrida, but his argument within any particular paper or article seems to hinge on the identification of a key, problematic term. His strategy is often to show that this particular term is crucial, pivotal and interesting in the argument of his protagonists. But then Derrida exposes the term as highly ambiguous, and that this ambiguity is important and reveals much about a philosophical problem. Such terms include *différance*, metaphor, archive, *pharmakon*, fraternity, signature, *maintenant* and *chora*. One of the keys to unlocking Derrida's line of reasoning in any of his articles is to be clear about the centrality of this target term in his argument.

As a final note by way of introduction to Derrida's thinking we should attend to the colour and timbre of Derrida's writing as it pertains to architecture. Many of the allusions and metaphors Derrida deploys are richly suggestive in the context of architecture, as is his use of evocative examples, tropes and metaphors (though they are never just that). In so writing he is in the company of other notable French thinkers: Jacques Lacan (1901–1981), Michel Foucault (1926–1984) and Gilles Deleuze (1925–1995). As well as copious literary, grammatical and typographic references, Derrida's essay titles and key words summon the world of the scriptorium, early printing presses, alchemical

Derrida's essay titles and key words summon the world of the scriptorium, early printing presses, alchemical laboratories, mechanical apparatus and richly material practices that might be connected with some baroque cabinet of curiosities or the studio of a Surrealist artist

laboratories, mechanical apparatus and richly material practices that might be connected with some baroque cabinet of curiosities or the studio of a Surrealist artist, and hence have potential as stimuli in the architectural design studio. As further indication of Derrida's enthusiasm for found objects (*objets trouvés*) or readymades, he led a high-profile protest against the dispersal of Surrealist

An architectural design studio.

leader André Breton's collection of artworks on the closing of Breton's workshop in 2003 (Motycka Weston, 2006). Derrida's philosophical 'readymades' include the *pharmakon* (pharmacy), the mystic writing pad (via Sigmund Freud), the postcard (via Jacques Lacan), the folded page, the glass column, hieroglyphics, tympanum (the hammer of the inner ear), the pyramid and mirror writing. Derrida's essay 'Tympanum' has an illustrated footnote to Vitruvius's water wheel (Derrida, 1982c). Though Derrida's earliest major work was on the origin of geometry (Derrida, 1989a), it has little to offer the architectural draftsman or CAD operator. In spite of the exotic nature of some of these allusions, in many ways Derrida's writing is informed by the everyday and the practical. As I indicate in the next chapter, the architectural reader can usefully approach Derrida from a very pragmatic point of view.

CHAPTER 1

Thinking about Architecture

For an architect the test of any philosophy is what difference it makes to the way architecture is practised, talked about, assessed and taught. In their professional lives architects need be concerned less with the question 'is it true?' than 'what practical difference does it make?' At least this is how I start to think about the philosophies and theories of thinkers such as Jacques Derrida for architects. In so doing I am advocating a mode of interrogation that is practical, that fits within a context of the practices of architecture: designing, documenting, building, reflecting, evaluating, interpreting, critiquing and defending, as well as formulating architectural histories and learning about architecture. I maintain that if we take Derrida's thinking seriously, then it makes a difference to the various practices of making architecture.

The Pragmatic philosopher Richard Rorty makes a pertinent observation in relating disciplines such as mathematics and philosophy to the practical sphere: 'Although some mathematics is obviously very useful to engineers, there's a lot of mathematics that isn't. Mathematics outruns engineering pretty quickly, and starts playing with itself' (Rorty, 1996b, p. 71). He says the same applies to philosophy in relation to politics: 'philosophy, we might say, outruns politics' (Rorty, 1996b, p. 71). I would add the same for philosophy and architecture. It is easy to get carried away with philosophy, that is, to be distracted from what we want to accomplish as architects by many fine philosophical distinctions and intricate disputes. We need sometimes to wrest Derrida's thought back to practice, though the practice of architecture is broader in its scope and conceits than engineering, if less theorised than politics.

How does Derrida's influence operate? Reading Derrida does not necessarily *cause* architects to change their practices. Think of paradigms or fields of practice, into which philosophical writings such as those of Derrida might intervene, as nodes within networks of influences, or gravitational fields within constellations. In an interview Derrida alludes to the way texts and other modes of creative production can interact, in this case in his relationship with the architect Peter Eisenman, an encounter to which I will return in Chapter 4.

> So I gave this text to Peter Eisenman and in his own way he started a project that was correlated with but at the same time independent of my text. That was true collaboration – not 'using' the other's work, not just illustrating or selecting from it … and so there is a kind of transparency or, I would say, a productive dialogue between the concerns, the styles, the person too.
>
> (Derrida, 1989b, p. 72)

Occasional correlations, independence, interdependence between transparent layers, dialogues, the merging of styles, interactions between personalities: these are the mechanisms by which philosophical texts and architecture exert their influences on one another.

Juxtapositions and oppositions

Aspects of architecture are already primed to receive Derrida's ways of thinking, particularly in so far as design ideas are stimulated by unusual juxtapositions. Studio-based architecture shares with much art and design a propensity to value the sideways look, the interpretation and practice that is off-the-wall, and for this legacy we can thank various movements, not least Dada, Surrealism, Russian Constructivism and Situationism. Unusual juxtaposition is simply the placement of one entity against another with which it does not necessarily belong. An umbrella against an umbrella stand would excite little interest, nor would the sight of a patient on an operating table, but place an umbrella on an operating table and you have something else. So the surrealist artist Max Ernst wrote that when the 'ready-made reality' of an umbrella is placed with that of a sewing machine on an operating table, the occasion provides the possibility for 'a new absolute that is true and poetic: the umbrella and the sewing machine will make love' (Breton, 1969, p. 275). The combination of disparate elements in this way has been likened to alchemy. Collages and montages of words, pictures and sounds function in much the same way, involving 'irrational' juxtapositions of ready-made elements. In architecture, Bernard Tschumi's conjectural studio project involving the building of a nightclub in a graveyard provides design stimulus that operates in a way similar to collage (Tschumi, 1994), or a designer could think of a swimming pool in a library, a train station that is also a television studio, a skyscraper as a grandfather clock.

The effectiveness of such juxtapositions is not a case simply of placing objects or ideas together in random fashion and thereby claiming an innovation. The context is crucial. In fact such juxtapositions can reveal much about context. The appreciation and reception of such juxtapositions requires that the artist-architect and the observer tunes in to what suits the moment, spatially, culturally and intellectually. Here the role of imagination, interpretation and judgement come into play, which return us to the practical: knowing what works in this situation and what doesn't. For example, it is usual, mundane and probably highly necessary to juxtapose a door with a wall, i.e. to position a door in a wall. Putting a door into the treads of a stair is less usual, but in the right context might be challenging or interesting, or even highly functional. To contemplate the insertion of a door in a wash basin would have little utility in an everyday housing project. Though thinking about a door in a bath might be appropriate where disability access is a concern.

A traditional logician or rationalist might want an explanation of how these processes of juxtaposition are generated and received, and how judgements are made. Perhaps there are rules about what goes with what, doors fit within walls, stairs connect storeys, roofs are at the tops of buildings. Perhaps there are rules pertaining to convention, by which the designer decides what is outside of convention. Deciding on what is inside and what is outside brings us to the role of oppositions. Juxtapositions of any interest play on the opposition, between what is and what is not, appropriate and inappropriate, true and false. Some linguists and cultural theorists would say that any explanation is oppositional through and through. You can't really reduce thought to something deeper, more rational or precise than the notion of the opposition. For the pragmatist the only thing that might precede the opposition is the primacy of human practice, the explanation of which requires appeal to yet further oppositions.

You can't really reduce thought to something deeper, more rational or precise than the notion of the opposition.

Totalising strategies

It is tempting to assume that sometimes there are oppositions, sometimes rules, sometimes imagination, sometimes continuities; all come into the rich play of meaning and interpretation. But there's a bolder and more interesting philosophical tactic at play here. It is more revealing to assert that rationality is completely oppositional, an assertion more satisfying to some philosophers than saying that rationality is sometimes oppositional and sometimes pertains to continua, or unities, or logical rules. Of course, there are many candidates for such totalising assertions: rationality could be rule-based, logical, mathematical, metaphorical, literal, interpretational, imaginary, in language, or playful. Can all such understandings be correct?

The theorist of play, Johan Huizinga, provides an interesting illustration of the human propensity to operate with totalities, i.e. to exaggerate. A small child rushes into the house and tells his mother he's just found a huge carrot. 'How big is it?' asks the mother. 'As big as God', comes the breathless reply. For Huizinga, 'The desire to make an idea as enormous and stupefying as possible is ... a typical play-function and is common both in child-life and in certain mental diseases' (Huizinga, 1955, p. 143). In other words, humans at their most basic like to go with the big idea and push it to extremes, a tendency Huizinga thinks we ought to restore. This totalising strategy reveals obvious contradictions, as if contrary to our experience everything must be made of carrots. To endorse a totalising view is perhaps a rhetorical strategy to force some issue, as if by advocating revolution as the only solution to the domination of capitalism, the social reformer Karl Marx (Marx, 1977) was overstating the cause of social justice to bring about some kind of more moderate social transformation.

The totalising view activates again the idea of the oppositional nature of thought. Rationality is all free play, or rationality is all rules. Surely, if it is not both in some measure then it is either one or the other. As an alternative the reflective critic could assert that you do not always have to decide between two views with totalising claims, but both can be held in parallel. The reflective architect can let them play against each other. The totalising view sets issues into intellectual conflict, the outcome of which is after all undecidable, including the verdict on their undecidability. I have already introduced such intellectual strategies in drawing attention to Derrida's oppositions of the absolute versus the relative, certainty versus contingency, order versus anarchy, the need for a centre versus assigning authority to the margins.

Agonistics

If all-encompassing views are a function of play then they are also a function of combat, heated argument and conflict in general. Oppositions can be conflictual and agonistic, a state we may want sometimes to conserve rather than resolve

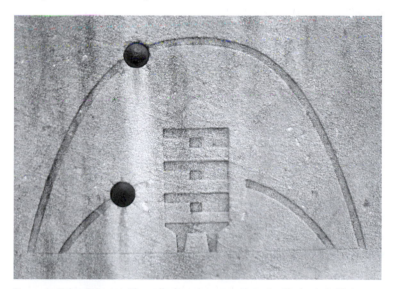

Forms in light. Solar motif on plinth at the entrance to Le Corbusier's Unite d'Habitation, Marseilles.

(Rendell, 2006, p. 9; Rawes, 2007). Not all oppositions in architecture seem immediately to entertain totalising claims: inside versus outside, structure versus ornament, service areas versus the areas served. But some positions are genuinely antagonistic, with adherents to one position refusing to consider the converse position. So professions tend to sign up to codes of ethics and would rarely entertain their converse (graft, self-interest, theft) as legitimate modes of professional practice. We only seek to do what is right and never knowingly what is wrong. As expounded by Le Corbusier, the early modernist conception of architecture as 'forms in light' did not entertain the priority of the converse of glowering shapes in the dark. Similarly, an architecture of simple purity does not entertain an architecture predicated on junk. Here, moving from one pole of an opposition to the other is only effected with an element of shock, painful effort, turmoil or anxiety, at least initially, as in Rem Koolhaas's celebration of 'junk spaces' (Koolhaas, 2004).

If the element of struggle is evident in the major oppositions then it may also pervade smaller, more localised polarities. Think of the difference between asserting that architecture is made of forms in light and declaring that architecture involves a contest between light and dark, or occupies the troubled place between noise and silence, saturation of the sensual field and total absence. Even the most prosaic oppositions of architecture can be cast in terms that indicate something is really at stake. This is Derrida for architects. There is always something at issue, and the stakes are high. Major as well as apparently minor oppositions are commonly treated as agonistic and problematic. One of Derrida's terms for the problematic condition is the *aporia*, a word in Ancient Greek relating to perplexity. For commentators on Derrida, such as John Caputo (Caputo, 1987; Derrida, 1993), this is the key to Derrida's thinking. The task is to keep perplexity and ambiguity alive rather than to resolve it. It is to show that any putative resolution is itself fraught with further ambiguity and complexity.

This is Derrida for architects. There is always something at issue, and the stakes are high.

Confounding oppositions

By most accounts Derrida is a master of careful and precise, though difficult, argumentation. There are many others who have sought to overturn convention, to upset certainties and to keep ambiguity in play. Whereas other intellectuals may resort to strident assertions, manifestos and slogans, Derrida focuses on close readings of texts and a critique of the verbal strategies of his opponents, often picking on those subtle and marginal strategies of which the targeted author may be unaware. Among his many accomplishments, Derrida had an enviable grasp of the whole philosophical tradition, as well as those of literature and art. His writing is steeped in references and allusions to the work of others, including those with whom he is in dispute. He unsettles his intellectual quarry by showing that the position an author is trying to assert or defend is already dependent on the very position the author is seeking to dispute. Derrida writes with self-confidence and alacrity, and at times seems also to be provoking and deliberately confounding his reader.

In summary, there is always something serious at stake in Derrida's arguments. He focuses on texts, worthy adversaries from philosophy and literature. His arguments involve oppositions and the priorities between them. As we shall see in the next chapter, he seeks to indicate how the privileged proposition in an opposition is in fact dependent on the lesser term, and he argues for a rehabilitation of the lesser term through its redefinition and reinstatement, generally involving a revision in terminology. In some respects there is a kind of formula to Derrida. Richard Rorty, pragmatic defender of Derrida's strategies, parodies this formulaic approach thus: 'Find something that can be made to look self-contradictory, claim that that contradiction is the central message of the text, and ring some changes on it' (Rorty, 1996a, p. 15). It concerned Derrida that the scholar can look to his work for such a formula. I contend that the extent to which architecture engages with oppositions and unusual juxtapositions it is primed to receive the thinking of Jacques Derrida.

CHAPTER 2

Language and Architecture

Derrida's early work dealt with the philosophical movement known as Phenomenology and the philosophy of its prime mover Edmund Husserl (Derrida, 1989a), who was in turn the teacher of Martin Heidegger (Heidegger, 1962; Sharr, 2006, 2007). It is reasonable therefore to think of Derrida as a student and critic of Phenomenology. However, his greatest impact pertains to theories of language, in particular Structuralism, the main subject of his seminal work *Of Grammatology* (Derrida, 1976). There are several very helpful texts that introduce language theories and Derrida's relationship to them, such as Terrence Hawkes' book *Structuralism and Semiotics* (1977), that explain Structuralism very clearly for a readership not already primed in language theory and philosophy. This helpful book also develops an account of *Post*structuralism as the successor to Structuralism and introduces Derrida's thinking. A further key explanatory text is Christopher Norris's *Deconstruction: Theory and Practice* (1982), which deals explicitly with the background to Derrida's thinking. Jonathan Culler's *On Deconstruction: Theory and Criticism after Structuralism* (1985) was apparently an influence on the architect Peter Eisenman, providing an introduction to Derrida's thinking. *The Prison House of Language*, by the prominent cultural theorist Fredric Jameson (1972), helps to situate Structuralism within wider cultural contexts. I draw substantially on these texts here. A further important text on language and architecture was published in 1969, entitled *Meaning in Architecture*, edited by Charles Jencks and George Baird. It predates the influence of Derrida and consists of a series of articles by architectural theorists. The main theories advanced there pertained to Structuralism, though the term 'semiotics' was also in vogue. Elsewhere I rehearse an explanation of language and Structuralism as they pertain to digital media and information technology (Coyne, 1995, 1999, pp. 120–134). Here I direct the arguments towards architecture.

Is architecture a language? There are prominent detractors from a linguistic view of architecture (Seligmann and Seligmann, 1977; Scruton, 1979; Donougho, 1987), but that there is even controversy on the issue provides evidence that language is a prominent architectural concern. So I start with an understanding of architecture as language. In so far as architects might appeal to the correct form, shape and configuration of a classical façade (Summerson, 1963) they are appealing to correctness and to grammar. In language as spoken and written there are recognisable and correct forms to sentences: words are categorised as nouns, verbs, adjectives, adverbs, articles and so on, and words have to be positioned relative to each other according to these categories. In English, adjectives generally precede the nouns to which they refer; every sentence ought to have a verb. Different languages and dialects exhibit diverse grammars. Perhaps architecture conforms similarly to conventions that can be recorded and analysed as grammars. Spaces get arranged relative to one another in certain ways: service spaces adjacent to the spaces served, bathrooms in a house should be close to bedrooms and forecourts appear in front of entrances (Alexander *et al.*, 1977).

A classical language of architecture. Palazzo Valmarana Braga, Vicenza by Andrea Palladio.

Students of architecture learn architecture's languages, and new recruits to an architectural firm adopt its way of identifying and arranging design elements. Designers might invent new spatial languages. Here concepts of style, grammar, convention, rule and formal and functional arrangement converge on concepts in language, specifically on the issue of syntax, the way sentences are put together.

But language features most prominently in architecture when we think of meaning, i.e. semantics. 'Design is the conscious effort to impose meaningful order', according to the design theorist Victor Papanek (1971, p. 3). It seems architects want to create or enhance meaningful, symbolically rich places that communicate. In any case artefacts, such as buildings, inevitably make reference to other objects, concepts, memories or places. Architecture seems to exhibit this language function of meaning and reference. Architecture displays the language function, as a medium for making reference, and buildings are objects to which reference is often made. In so far as Derrida's thinking has something to say about meaning and language it is pertinent to architecture.

Derrida's strategy is often termed *Deconstruction*, a term that he introduced in *Of Grammatology*. Derrida states that the apparent rationality of a text inaugurates the 'destruction, not the demolition but the de-sedimentation, the de-construction' of its own argumentation (1976, p. 10). The term 'Deconstruction' clearly presents in opposition to concepts of construction, or at least, structure. There are architectural connotations here, but the most direct reference from Deconstruction is to Structuralism, the highly influential movement in language and cultural theory. Deconstruction has also been termed Poststructuralism. So to understand Derrida it is necessary to grasp what is meant by Structuralism.

to understand Derrida it is necessary to grasp what is meant by Structuralism.

Language and history

The earliest formal and rigorous study of language is generally attributed to Ferdinand de Saussure (1857–1913), the Swiss-French scholar whose lecture notes on language were published in 1916 under the title *Course in General Linguistics*. Prior to that time language was a diffuse study that mainly came under the heading of *philology*. Philology was a historical study that primarily focused on texts and their interpretation and translation, rather than language as spoken. Comparative philology was concerned with the relationships between languages, that is, with the lineage of language, how one language derives from another, in the same way that botanists might observe how one plant species appears to have evolved from another. This historicisation of language was never far from the proposition that there might have existed an original language, from which others derived. So the philologist William Jones (1746–1794) noted that Sanskrit had a 'more perfect structure than the Greek, more copious than the Latin, and more exquisitely refined than either', an observation that points to them having an elusive 'common source' (Harris, 1999, p. 3). The French social theorist, Jean-Jacques Rousseau (1712–1778), to whom Derrida makes frequent reference, wrote a major *Essay on the Origin of Language* in which he describes the characteristics of this hypothetical originary language of 'images, feelings, and figures' (Rousseau, 1966, p. 15). Though few would argue for the existence of a primary language (or primary languages) now, the study of language change, or how one language or dialect relates to and evolves from another, is still of interest in historical linguistics (McMahon, 1994).

But Saussure sought to depart from this historical emphasis, highlighting the importance of the structures common to languages and across languages and language groups. He drew an analogy with a game of chess (Saussure, 1983, p. 88), observing that the state on the chessboard is sufficient to inform the casual observer of the state of play, or even of the next best move. The state of play depends only on the current relationships on the board. You do not need to observe the history of moves that brought the play to its current state. As is the case with chess, language too is about relationships within the whole system at any point in time. In any case, language change is inevitably piecemeal, and to focus on the details of sequential evolution misses the sets of relationships that constitute the bigger picture of how language functions.

So Saussure departed from the orthodoxy of his day by proposing that the synchronic (time independent or parallel) dimension to language is more revealing than its diachronic dimension. The diachronic, or historical, study of language focuses on the way languages change in time and how languages are derived from each other. To study the synchronicity of language is to look at the structures within any particular language, the relationships within the language, at a point in its evolution and compare it with the structures of other languages. So different languages have structural similarities that seem to transcend the particularities of individual sound patterns and local grammatical differences. For Saussure, we learn more by examining the current state of all languages, a slice through the world's languages, or rather similarities and differences in the multiplicity of the world's languages at any moment (such as at the present moment), than by looking at the derivations of languages.

So the Saussurean approach to language is regarded as Structuralist. It is concerned with the synchronic study of language independently of how any particular language might have evolved. Structuralism is a movement in language theory and cultural theory that takes to heart the importance of the structures in language, and is already sceptical towards notions of lineage and origins, a scepticism shared and developed later on by Derrida.

The linguistic orthodoxy against which Saussure was opposed has parallels with the way that eighteenth- and nineteenth-century theorists thought about architecture. In so far as we think of architecture as language then there are lessons about its history. The architectural historian Joseph Rykwert provides an account of the propensity within architectural discourse to appeal to the origins of architecture (Rykwert, 1997), evident in the writings of Vitruvius (Vitruvius, 1960) through to Laugier (Laugier, 1977) and Ruskin (Ruskin, 1956). According to a common architectural mythology, the originating architectural artefact is the 'primitive hut', that elusive primary moment of architectural invention, the traces of which persist overtly in the classical orders and the Gothic, and, on close analysis, in remnant form elsewhere. The hut is the architectural prototype, fashioned from the trunks of trees, which become columns. The tree canopy becomes the roof, and then the whole assembly is mimicked in stone. There are other stories about the origins of architecture. The rationalist educator, Jean Nicolas Louis Durand (1796–1886), developed an alternative to Laugier's story based on 'utility', to which end he developed a derivational typology of built forms (Durand, 2000). Durand's book shows the evolution of the cathedral from the simple Basilica form, over successive generations, based on functional shifts. In so far as architecture looks back to its origins and thinks about its own evolution it participates in a kind of diachronic analysis, as opposed to a synchronic analysis that prefers taking what we have now and in the record and analysing its relationships. This is not to criticise the necessity to understand and develop architectural histories, but rather to denounce architectural *Historicism*, a kind of belief in the progress and evolution of architecture from the simple to the more advanced, that there is a 'purpose' to history, including the idea that each age has a 'spirit' to which architecture gives expression (Runes, 1942, p. 127), a view subject to critique by the philosopher of science Karl Popper and architectural theorist David Watkin (Popper, 1957; Watkin, 1977). Derrida is clearly heir to this scepticism about Historicism, that there can be purpose to history, and that cultural phenomena such as architecture can be traced back to an origin.

Correspondence

Saussure also tackles the convention of his day that words relate to actual things in some external reality. The early scholar and theologian Augustine (354–430) thought that when children learn to speak they are in fact memorising from people around them the association between a spoken word and an object, that is, they give 'a name to an object' (Augustine, 1991, p. 18). This correspondence theory has been branded 'the most archaic language theory of all' (Jameson, 1972, p. 30). The naming operations of language are easily challenged when the language user realises that there are so many concepts, ideas and objects to which words might refer that are not tangible, discrete or physical (e.g. red, five, strong). Saussure discusses problems in identifying precisely what are the 'immediately recognizable concrete units' in science, history and grammar. As the Structuralist commentator Frederick Jameson points out, relativity theories and then quantum physics pose problems for the correspondence view. In the case of the conflict between the wave and particle theories of light, for example, Jameson notes that 'scientific investigation has reached the limits of perception; its objects are no longer things or organisms which are isolated by their own physical structures from each other, and which can be dissected and classified in various ways' (1972, p. 14).

In spite of there being no tangible referent in an external reality outside of language, language seems to work. We humans make ourselves understood and we accomplish tasks with the aid of language. Social groups learn how to use words in particular contexts. Perhaps after all language has less to do with correspondences and an independent reality than with usage (Wittgenstein, 1953). According to Saussure, the linkage between word and thing has no particular foundation. It is decided by the consensus of a language community. So the word 'house' bears no special relationship to that entity built on the side of the street other than what convention allows, as is evident from the fact that there are different words available for the same object in different languages. The relationship between word and object is therefore 'arbitrary' and the thing being referred to (the house) is not so much an object as a concept. Saussure's radical position about language and reality can be summed up by his proposition: 'A linguistic sign is not a link between a thing and a name, but between a concept and a sound pattern' (Jameson, 1972, p. 66). So Saussure provides a systematic way of studying language which does not require that language appeal to a reality beyond itself.

Structuralist language theorists therefore attach great importance to the problematic of this relationship between the *signifier* and the *signified*, sometimes represented as an equation or ratio, with 'signifier' positioned over a horizontal line and with 'signified' below that, implying the priority of one over the other. Commonly the two terms are separated by a forward slash (separatrix), '/', a symbol that reverberates throughout Structuralist writing.

The psychoanalytic philosopher Jacques Lacan seems at times to treat the relationship as a mathematical fraction S/s, with variants (Lacan, 1979). The relationship between the signifier and the signified is often referred to as the 'sign situation', which is already a departure from the common view that language consists of signs that refer to things. For Structuralism, the sign situation implicates the signifier and the thing signified in a system of signs.

The relationship between the signifier and the signified is often referred to as the 'sign situation', which is already a departure from the common view that language consists of signs that refer to things.

At first reading, and for some of its detractors, Structuralism seems to deny the existence of reality and is therefore against common sense (Sokal and Bricmont, 2003). Structuralism does not deny the presence of objects to which language might make reference (signifieds), but it implies a resonance between language as a whole and the whole that is human experience. According to Jameson, Structuralism maintains that it is the whole language system that 'lies parallel to reality itself' rather than the individual word or sentence that represents or 'reflects' the individual object or event in the everyday world of experience. It is the entire system of signs 'which is analogous to whatever organized structures exist in the world of reality'. Our understanding through language 'proceeds from one whole, or Gestalt to the other, rather than on a one-to-one basis' (Jameson, 1972, p. 33). As a further advocate of this Structuralist realism, Roland Barthes asserts that language 'is not expected to *represent* reality, but to signify it' (1973, p. 149). So Structuralism lays stress on signs and language rather than empirical realities. Needless to say, Derrida is heir to the Structuralist scepticism towards the concept that language operates by making reference to an independent reality outside of language, the correspondence theory of language. In fact, as we shall see Derrida goes further than Structuralism by demonstrating that the referent (signified) in any language statement is elusive, or at least it is part of a chain of references.

In so far as we think of architecture as a language then the elusive nature of the referent (signified) is demonstrated even more starkly than in the case of words. To what do the volutes on the ionic capital of a nineteenth-century neo-classical building refer: a rolled leaf, a Greek temple, grandeur, Renaissance ideals, or other Victorian buildings? It probably references all of these, or something else, depending on context.

Sign systems and difference

As linguists focus on the synchronicity of language it is the structures that become important, rather than individual elements. According to the developmental psychologist Jean Piaget (1896–1980), Structuralism 'adopts from the start a relational perspective, according to which it is neither the elements nor a whole that comes about in a manner one knows not how, but the relations amongst elements that count' (Piaget, 1970, pp. 8–9). The idea of 'the relationship' is very important in Saussure's linguistics.

As I have shown, a linguistic sign is made up of signifier and signified relationships. An instance of such a relationship makes up a linguistic sign, and the multiplicity of such relationships makes up a system of signs. The relationship that Saussure focused on was the simple relationship between sound patterns. What is the key relationship between the enormous collection of sound patterns that make up the lexicon of a language? Sound patterns operate by virtue of *difference*, a term that was to become emblematic for Derrida, as indicated in the Prologue. Saussure begins his explanation of difference with the phoneme, the basic constituent of sound patterns. Language works because we are able to distinguish one phoneme from another: 'The sound of a word is not in itself important, but the phonetic contrasts which allow us to distinguish that word from any other. That is what carries the meaning' (Saussure, 1983, p. 116). So the word 'house' is different from 'mouse', and many other words that are otherwise similar, because of the distinctiveness in this case of the initial phoneme (Jakobson and Halle, 1956).

Saussure's analysis, and that of his linguistic expositors and critics, on the theme of difference is detailed, and may not appear directly relevant to architecture. For example, as evidence for the importance of difference in language he cites the case of the French *r* sound. As there is no *ch* sound (as in Bach) in common French usage, it would be possible to substitute *r* for *ch* and still be understood. According to Saussure that would not work in German however, as the *ch* sound already exists. If every *r* sound became a *ch* then one of the major ways of discriminating between words in German would be lost (Saussure, 1983, p. 117). In other words, language communities make optimal use of the lexicon of sounds they have available, and use these sounds to mark out distinctions in meaning. In similar vein, where there are several words available then speakers will deploy these to mark out differences of meaning. So through the historical introduction of French words English has two words, *sheep* and *mutton*, that are deployed to denote the living animal and the culinary version respectively. In French the single word *mouton* must cover both meanings (Saussure, 1983, p. 114). An author who has inspected an online thesaurus to find the right word for a particular context knows that a plethora of synonyms generates a wealth of fine distinctions.

What constitutes difference, or at least a meaningful difference, again depends on the conventions of the particular language community. Being able to speak and understand Japanese relies on a certain set of phonemic differences that are scarcely recognised as differences by native English speakers. The same applies to comparisons between any two languages, such as English and French, as in the difference between the French word *pas* and *par*. According to the idea of phonemic difference, only differences that have developed as important in the language are registered. Others might constitute peculiarities of accent or dialect, or go unnoticed.

The language we use to describe architecture exhibits a similar propensity to enable or reflect differences that are of practical importance. For example, we readily talk about the front of a house and the back of a house, but a house also often has two sides. There is no unambiguous phrase for easily distinguishing the two sides of a house – right and left, east and west? One might presume that the differences between the front and back of something are so important to get right that we have clearly different terms for them. In architecture we do not only deal in words. Designers may also deploy different architectural elements or materials at the front and back of a house. Language, and architecture, could be seen in various ways to operate with distinctions and differences that operate in the context of one another. As a further example, in New Zealand it is relatively common for middle-class families to own a second home. Such a home may be called a 'bach' (short for 'bachelor home') if it is a small-scale residence for occasional occupation. If it is larger and for family use then it may be called a 'beach house'. The geographical, economic and social conditions of that particular place engender a set of discriminations that are other than what one would see in the United Kingdom, where such a distinction (between a bach and a beach house) would be less relevant to social conditions. Such distinctions in naming are manifested further in the design and configuration of such building types. Difference is manifested in the establishment of oppositions in both language as spoken and architecture as language: front/back, centre/periphery, inside/outside, structure/ornament. Systems of differences operate as the means by which communities make discriminations. For Saussure:

> *In the language itself, there are only differences.* **Even more important than that is the fact that, although in general a difference presupposes positive terms between which the difference holds, in a language there are only differences, and** *no positive terms.*
>
> (1983, p. 149)

As we have already seen, Derrida seizes on the concept of difference as a kind of foundation to language, but a foundation that is indeterminate, ambiguous and unsettling.

Deep structure

The notion of language as a system of relationships, predicated on difference, suggested to Saussure that there are two aspects to language. There is the superficial or surface structure of language as it appears in any particular culture, the *parole* of language, language as it is spoken (or written) subject to local variation. But there is a structure underlying the different languages we encounter that is the *langue*. *Parole* is the active, *langue* is the passive and abiding dimension of speech. Issues of local accent, mispronunciation and personal style are matters for the 'science of *parole*' (Jameson, 1972, pp. 26–27). But Saussure is more concerned with the *langue*, that which exceeds the local, the structures beneath the peculiarities of specific uses of individual languages. There are connections here with architecture. In the case of a particular building we may think of the cladding, choice of finishes, fittings and signage as the surface structure. The form of the building, including its structure and general plan form, constitutes the deep structure. The surface elements could be removed without affecting the form. By an alternative reading, the surface structure pertains to mere appearances, while the deep structure could be the intentions, meanings and ideas present in a work of architecture.

The surface/depth distinction also resonates with common views in psychology that equate deep structure with the unconscious, either collective or private (Davis, 1997). Here Derrida's thinking exhibits a major departure from Structuralism as he avoids any endorsement of concepts such as deep meanings, authentic understanding, unconscious desires or other metaphysical constructs. He describes the related distinction between the conscious and the unconscious as 'a very crude tool for dealing with relations in and to language' (Derrida, 1981, p. 96). In so far as there is ever a deep structure, a foundation, a more profound, enduring or more structured substrate to language, human psychology or architecture, Derrida shows this to be in flux, indeterminate and in fact no foundation at all.

In so far as there is ever a deep structure, a foundation,

a more profound, enduring or more structured substrate to

language, human psychology or architecture, Derrida shows

this to be in flux, indeterminate and in fact no foundation at

all.

Widening the scope of language

It would be difficult to apply some of these technicalities of structural linguistics specifically to architecture were it not for the insights of anthropology. One of the contributions of Structuralism has been to open a space for considering language other than as spoken and written communication. For example, in the writing of the cultural theorist Roland Barthes, Structuralism admits art, fashion, architecture, sport and culture generally as forms of language (Barthes, 1973, p. 118). Even if we think of architecture as other than a language, then in Structuralist terms it is certainly *like* a language, not least in that it is susceptible to discussion in terms of oppositions, a point I emphasised in the previous chapter. In so far as architecture can be accessed through concepts of the opposition, it can be discussed in terms of Structuralist language theory.

in the writing of the cultural theorist Roland Barthes,

Structuralism admits art, fashion, architecture, sport and

culture generally as forms of language

The anthropologist Claude Lévi-Strauss (1908–2009) developed Structuralism as a mode of research for examining kinship patterns, taboos, culinary practices, ritual, marriage laws and so on (Lévi-Strauss, 1963). Structuralist anthropology

Clothing as language. Fashion mannequins. Open-air market, Rabat, Morocco.

simplifies the matter of phonemic difference. The equivalents of phonemic
binary differences are concepts such as clean and unclean, cooked and raw,
male and female, in and out, young and old, heaven and earth, life and death
and so on. So members of a traditional village community may think of
themselves in terms of their descent from animals; one group regarding
themselves as descendants of bears, while members of another community see
themselves as descended from wolves. Community X is as different from
community Y as are two different animal species. Wolves, bears or eagles may
equally suffice to establish this understanding of difference, which is caught up
in the myriad ways community X deals with those outside the community. Lévi-
Strauss calls this practice of taking whatever is available from the local
conditions for the *parole* of a language community '*bricolage*'.

When anthropological study is opened up in this way then we see that similar
structural distinctions are made in modern societies with their own regional
applicability, which are in some cases equally dependent on distinctions
between animal species, as in sports: tigers, lions, bulldogs (Hawkes, 1977,

pp. 54–55). Lévi-Strauss also develops a theory of transformation: 'mythic thought always progresses from the awareness of oppositions towards their resolution' (1963, p. 224), and there are rules of transformation that bring about a shift from one variant of a myth to another (Hawkes, 1977, p. 48).

We can see the implications of the Structuralist position in the development of architecture, and Structuralism has provided an important contribution to understanding traditional architectures. For example, in the case of a Romanesque church, one discerns a layout and symbol system pertaining to the cycles of the sun, the moon and the zodiac. From a Structuralist perspective one could analyse these peculiarities of Romanesque churches in terms of an intricate matrix of oppositions: east and west, light and dark, past and future, time and space, life and death, heaven and earth, transience and eternity, centre and periphery. In so doing we would find similar structural relationships in the layout of the Forbidden City of Beijing, a Hindu temple or the layout of a Pawnee earth lodge (Snodgrass, 1990).

Perhaps it is easy enough to identify and analyse traditional architectures in Structuralist terms, to which the language of deep structures might seem appropriate, but obtain less to the global, self-aware and knowingly self-referential world of contemporary architecture, to which Poststructuralism more readily applies. Derrida is a key figure in this radicalisation of Structuralism.

Radicalising Structuralism

Structuralism has its detractors and critics, not least among sociologists who claim that Structuralism seems to deny any priority to the concept of agency and hence social responsibility (Giddens, 1984, p. 32). Structuralism readily submits to the promotion of self-referential language games, and its own internal economy of signs and reference, without actually alighting on the practical. Structuralism has also institutionalised its own critique as Poststructuralism (and Deconstruction), which can be seen to further radicalise Structuralism's key insights, particularly through the work of Roland Barthes (1915–1980), Michel Foucault (1926–1984) and of course Jacques Derrida. In *Of Grammatology*,

Derrida focuses on destabilising certain Structuralist concepts of language, in particular the signifier–signified relationship. Derrida argues at length, as was already implicit in Structuralism, that the signified (referent) constantly evades identification in any particular language situation. It is rather the case that signifiers appear to be referring constantly to other signifiers, and in turn these connect to further signifiers. So the word (signifier) 'house' may not simply point to the house on the street, a single concept of house, but to the image of a house, or a picture in a magazine, or a house in a popular TV sitcom or soap opera, an advertising brochure, a poem, or to hearth, sustenance, family, or even the gesture by which I emphasise the act of signification (pointing); and each of these signifiers directs the speaker or listener to some other signifier.

When a speaker makes an utterance, the end point of such a referential chain is commonly identified as the meaning of the utterance, but in so far as meaning resides anywhere it is in the trace left by these chains of signification. There is no final point on which anything resembling a meaning might alight. One of Derrida's most revealing metaphors is of the postal service, the implications of which to concepts of meaning he develops and exhausts in his book *The Postcard* (Derrida, 1979), in particular if we recall that messages may get returned to their sender, arrive late, be lost in transit, lose their context, convey unfulfilled promises, be misread, and confuse meaning rather than clarify. Like the postal service, language is a kind of circulation system that keeps things in play and leaves in its wake a multiplicity of connections and referents. Language can only function and always has, through the concept of trace. Barthes asserts 'there always remains, around the final meaning, a halo of virtualities where other possible meanings are floating' (1973, p. 143). For Derrida (and Barthes) this endless referentiality is the norm, and any language situation in which we simply ascribe *this* signifier to *that* signified is a highly contextual and transient instance of ascription.

Meaning and metaphysics

For Derrida, the notion of meaning in language shares the metaphysical problematic to which I alluded in the Prologue about supposed foundations to knowledge. Meanings and foundations are in fact non-determinate phenomena that are constantly in flux and play. As with meaning, it is not that there is no centre, core or foundation to any phenomenon, but that the core or ground relies on other conditions to establish itself as a ground. Hence Derrida's reference to the 'bottomless chessboard' on which certainties are founded (Derrida, 1982a, p. 22) to which I referred in the Prologue. The centre relies on what is supposed to be built around it. Alternatively, the centre is always 'foreign'. It is something brought in from outside, by definition without justification, to found something new and different to what was there before. The concept of foundation seems to rely on this instability to establish its status as a core. Meaning is similarly caught in this indeterminate play.

This is one of the major implications of Derrida's thinking for architecture, in bringing together issues of meaning and questions of metaphysics and showing the dependence of each on conditions of uncertainty and undecidability. Derrida therefore informs architecture in three ways. First, his thinking on language is informative in its own right, reminding us that the deep structures, tenets, foundations and bases of architecture are open to question. Second, as we shall see in the next chapter, the process by which Derrida arrives at such conclusions reveals much about language, meaning, reason, human understanding and, therefore, design. Third, architecture is required to resort to apparatuses other than authoritative meanings on which to peg its claims to expertise. In so far as architecture's appeals to the authority of particular meanings, methods, knowledge, expertise, science and genius are metaphysical, they are insufficient. Derrida shifts the discussion from either certainty or despair towards the necessity to keep talking, to keep language live rather than trapped in an unwieldy edifice of fixed definitions, to keep questioning, challenging, revising and being open to surprise, themes to be developed in the chapters that follow.

CHAPTER 3

Intertextuality and Metaphor

Derrida adopts an intriguing strategy in presenting the case for a new view of language and metaphysics that draws on the tenets of Structuralism. In the process he reveals an approach to argumentation, reading texts, communication and intellectual development that extends to other areas of creativity, including architecture.

Derrida outlines his case in his book *Of Grammatology* (Derrida, 1976), but also in his lengthy essay 'Plato's Pharmacy', which is effectively a critique of Platonism, and a commentary on Plato's *Phaedrus*, a dialogue between Socrates, Plato's teacher, and a young pupil, Phaedrus. This Platonic dialogue is ostensibly about the exercise of true wisdom, through reason, against the shallow and beguiling rhetorical strategies of the Sophists, with their appeal to mythic stories and persuasive trickery. The vehicle for Plato's endorsement of reason is a series of three speeches about love. 'Orthodox' commentaries on *Phaedrus*, such as that by Robin Waterfield, the translator of the Oxford edition of *Phaedrus* (Plato, 2002), generally draw attention to its lessons on the nature of rhetoric; its vindication of Plato's method of writing, as a series of conversations between protagonists (dialectic), and the divided passions of the human psyche (a pre-Freudian version of the ego, the id and the superego); and the obvious and the exclusive recourse to male erotic relationships in exemplifying love. In his essay 'Plato's Pharmacy', Derrida takes a completely different tack from orthodox commentary and concentrates instead on a passage in *Phaedrus* recounting a myth of the origin of writing.

Before examining this passage in the *Phaedrus* we note therefore that Derrida's focus through his works centres on the importance of the relationship between written words, on parchment and paper, and words as spoken. It need hardly be stated that many scholars, from Plato onwards, have exercised great skills in writing, in putting ideas on paper and communicating them across the generations. We live in a culture of the written and printed word. For most thinkers on the subject, this intellectual and social achievement, of preserving and transmitting ideas by writing and print, comes at a cost. In writing things down, displaying text on a computer screen, or printing to paper, human beings effectively fix statements down, thereby relinquishing the power and immediacy of the spoken word, whether we think of speaking as the delivery of an oration, a lecture, a radio broadcast, mumbling to oneself or engaging in animated conversation. This lament about the loss of the immediacy of conversation and chatter is well expressed by Marshall McLuhan (McLuhan, 1962), pioneering media theorist of the 1960s and to whose work Derrida makes passing references (Derrida, 1982b, p. 329). For McLuhan, the invention of writing asserted priority to the eye and the capability of vision. Under the sway of written texts, humankind sees things written down, and at a distance, and so derives notions of objectivity and the methods of science. But before the cataclysmic invention of writing, human communities were permeated by speech and chatter and, of course, listening, the culture of the ear. Drawing loosely from anthropological studies, McLuhan's mythic construction of this epochal transition characterises aural culture as altogether more engaged, absorbed and undifferentiated than the subsequent civilising influence of visual culture.

McLuhan extends this myth to the current condition. Electronic media, with its ceaseless babble of voices, augurs a kind of return to the immediacy of the aural tribe. Think of the prevalence of sound and voice in portable transistor radios in the 1960s, personal stereos and now mobile phones. I explore these propositions in relation to contemporary digital media elsewhere (Coyne, 1995, 1999, 2008). Much of the celebration and justification of new electronic media, and the hope that they enable the restoration of community (through social media such as Facebook and Twitter), is founded on a hope for a return to the immediacy and dialectical nature of the aural over the visual. The problematic relationship between the written and the spoken word is explored at length in the writings of scholars such as Eric Havelock and Walter Ong (Havelock, 1986; Ong, 2002).

For our purposes here it is sufficient to note that dating back as far as Plato, the philosophical literature harbours an awareness and suspicion of the power of the written word and a nostalgia for a pre-literate condition. This is no more evident than in Plato's retelling of the myth of the origin of writing in *Phaedrus*. The story recounts several reservations to the teaching of skills in writing, addressed to the Egyptian god Theuth, the putative inventor of writing:

> **It will atrophy people's memories. Trust in writing will make them remember things by relying on marks made by others, from outside themselves, not on their own inner resources, and so writing will make the things they have learnt disappear from their minds. Your invention is a potion for jogging the memory, not for remembering. You provide your students with the appearance of intelligence, not real intelligence. Because your students will be widely read, though without contact with a teacher, they will seem to be men of wide knowledge, when they will usually be ignorant.**
>
> **(Plato, 2002, p. 69, l. 275a)**

These words appear as part of a dialogue and are put into the mouth of Plato's teacher Socrates (i.e. the story of Theuth and writing is told by Socrates), who famously never wrote anything down. Derrida references this passage from *Phaedrus* in his extended essay ('Plato's Pharmacy').

Derrida also refers extensively to Rousseau. In his essay 'On the Origins of Language', Rousseau claims that writing 'crystallizes language': 'It changes not the words but the spirit, substituting exactitude for expressiveness', and further, 'In writing, one is forced to use all the words according to their conventional meaning. But in speaking, one varies the meanings by varying ones tone of voice, determining them as one pleases' (1966, pp. 21–22). Speech is an altogether more expressive medium than writing, which is to say, closer to the thoughts of the discussants.

Rousseau's reservations about writing extend to his personal life. He indicates in his autobiography how he preferred to hide behind his writing.

> I would enjoy society as much as the next man, if I were not certain to show myself there not only to my own disadvantage, but as quite different from what I am. The decision I took to write and to hide myself away was precisely the right one for me. Had I been more visible, no one would ever have known what I was worth, would not even have suspected it.

> (2008, p. 114)

Through this self-confessed shyness, delivered no doubt with a portion of false modesty, Rousseau was able to hide behind his writing and only expose himself as he wanted to be seen, through writing. So writing has this character of concealing the truth about ourselves, the truth of the author or the would-be speaker.

Saussure similarly valorises the spoken over the written as the basis for understanding language, presenting the value of the immediate linkage between 'a concept and a sound pattern' (Jameson, 1972, p. 66). As illuminated by Derrida, these and other expressions about language indicate a common perception: that, for all its power and achievement, to write things down as texts, to store them in libraries and on databases and to transmit and circulate texts is only a substitute for the real thing, which is direct and unmediated communication between human beings (Derrida, 1982b, p. 312). Ideas only form as we speak in conversation, speaking and listening connect directly with who we are, utterances are of the authentic moment, provisional, contextual, open to refinement and adjustment. Derrida disagrees precisely with this common perception.

Writing as a drug

Derrida titles his essay on *Phaedrus* 'Plato's Pharmacy' in response to a term in the quotation from the *Phaedrus* given above about the origins of writing: 'Your invention is a potion for jogging the memory, not for remembering' (Plato, 2002, p. 69, l. 275a). Derrida makes much of the word 'potion', variously rendered by different translators of *Phaedrus* as 'medicine', 'antidote', 'drug' and 'poison'. It seems that the original Greek word, *pharmakon*, can be translated either as something that cures or that on the contrary makes you

Antique pharmacy sign at Piazza delle Erbe adjacent to Andrea Palladio's
Basilica, Vicenza, Italy.

unwell, an ambiguity that appears reasonable as early medical practice was at
best a risky business (Mikics, 2010, p. 148).

Derrida puts considerable emphasis on the difficulties translators have had with
the word *pharmakon* and its various associations. And here Derrida's
commentators see his essay as revealing much about his strategy of analysis
variously described as 'intertextual'. Derrida traces the word *pharmakon* and its
variants through other Platonic writings. One of the variant forms is
pharmakeus, which relates to a magician, and a scapegoat. The Athenians
apparently kept outcasts, who might also be illegal practitioners of black arts,
within their midst so that they could be sacrificed in the event of calamity.

> the representative of the outside is nonetheless *constituted*, regularly granted
> its place by the community, chosen, kept, fed, etc., in the very heart of the
> inside. These parasites were as a matter of course domesticated by the living
> organism that housed them at its expense.
>
> (Derrida, 1981, p. 133)

In keeping with so many of Derrida's reversals, it transpires that the core, the centre, the safe haven is also the source of disquiet and corruption. The sanctuary harbours the very entities it seeks to exclude, and for its own purpose. There are implications here about domestic and city life in particular and social conditions in general. *Pharmakon* also means colour, according to Derrida (1981, p. 140). It is the cosmetic used to make corpses presentable prior to burial (Derrida, 1981, p. 142). Elsewhere Plato denigrates painting as a derived form of copying, several removes from the original object it represents, which in turn is but a pale copy of the ideal object resident in the realm of the ideas, the Intelligible.

So Derrida's strategy in 'Plato's Pharmacy' is to establish through all these examples intertextual connections and traces, that writing is in fact denigrated, as a poison, but that this is a highly ambiguous condition. The turning point in Derrida's argument hinges on his identification of a section in *Phaedrus* where Socrates and his student agree that the right way of using words is where words are 'written along with knowledge in the soul of a student'. This is the 'living,

Pharmacological paraphernalia on a shelf in the design studio.

ensouled speech of a man of knowledge' and 'the written word is a mere image of this' (Plato, 2002, p. 70, l. 276a). So if conventional wisdom claims that the act of speaking is closest to the mind, soul, of the human being, then this inner being is already permeated by concepts of writing (on the soul). Derrida observes that in order to describe what is special and authentic about speech, Plato has to resort to the metaphor of words as written in the soul. It seems that it is always necessary to describe what is good, the privileged entity in an opposition (speech in this case) by recourse to the lesser term (writing).

Writing in the soul is therefore a kind of proto-writing, a more basic and primordial written entity, but writing nonetheless. Derrida concedes that 'writing in the soul' is a metaphor. It is important therefore for Derrida to establish that metaphors are not merely ornaments to language, a proposition that warrants further diversion: 'Metaphoricity is the logic of contamination and the contamination of logic' (1981, p. 149). There is no escaping metaphor. In his article 'White mythology: Metaphor in the context of philosophy', Derrida indicates how metaphor challenges the concept of the pure, literal idea to which any metaphor is supposed to refer. Metaphor is 'an accomplice of that which it threatens' (1974, p. 73). Metaphor contaminates the literal. Neither is there any escaping the contamination of the good from the bad: good writing versus bad writing, speech as a good thing versus writing as a bad thing. For Derrida, 'the good one can be designated only through the metaphor of the bad one' (1981, p. 149). Here again Derrida demonstrates the alacrity of his intertextual strategy, threading together themes such as language, writing, metaphor, contamination and value (the good), admittedly often to the frustration of the novice reader.

Proto-writing

In *Of Grammatology*, and resorting to less colourful metaphors, Derrida explains further the characteristics of proto-writing (1976, p. 57). The way linguists describe how language operates draws inevitably on how people communicate via writing. Communication in language seems to involve signs, whether uttered, gestured, drawn or written. Signs operate through difference as explained by Saussure. Second, these signs are repeatable. They can be reproduced: drawings and written words can be copied. Third, sign sequences can be disseminated. Sequences of signs can be recognised as the same even in different circumstances. It is therefore possible to pass sign sequences on from one situation to another. Fourth, sign sequences operate in the absence of an originator. It is possible to quote the sign sequence to a third party without the presence of the originator and without knowing that person's situation or intentions. The sign sequence is capable of signifying even when uttered, stored or presented independently of intention.

According to Derrida, the way people communicate with written texts presents as the model of all communication: difference, reproduction, repetition, dissemination and operating at a distance from the author. In other words, these features of communication are usually the features we associate with writing. Written texts can be copied and repeated, they can be distributed and passed from one person to another, the originator does not need to be present for them to signify.

Derrida indicates that exactly the same processes are claimed of unwritten speech as are claimed of writing. A spoken utterance can be repeated by someone other than the originator. It is possible to disseminate a spoken speech to a crowd. Utterances can be passed on by 'word of mouth'. The original speaker does not need to be present. The conveyor of the utterance does not have to understand the utterance in order for a third party to receive and make sense of the spoken words. We commonly recite poetry we do not understand, and the poem loses nothing of its power to signify when recited. Choristers can sing in Latin without knowing what the words mean. Actors and orators commonly rote-learn and recite sign sequences without the mediation of intention. The features of sign, repetition, distribution and absence are commonly regarded as attributes of writing, but apply equally to speech.

The conventional view is that people commit to writing what they have spoken, or want to speak, implying writing is a mere, imperfect vehicle for the spoken word. So Derrida reverses this opposition by claiming that the way we describe speech depends after all on the way we describe writing. Clearly infants do not learn to write before they can speak, and there exist cultures where spoken communication takes place without writing. But for Derrida there exists something that precedes, chronologically and in terms of importance, something before either speech or writing, and this prior entity bears all the trappings of writing, as a proto-writing. It would miss the point to demand evidence for such a proto-writing outside of language. For Derrida, rather than embark on an empirical search for such an entity it is sufficient to scrutinise texts, via his intertextual analysis that reveals the presence of writing everywhere, especially when its importance is denigrated, as in Plato's *Phaedrus* or Rousseau's *Confessions*.

So Derrida's argument begins with the distinction between speech, the privileged term, against writing, the denigrated or supplemental term. He shows that in the very texts that assert this difference and priority, the tables can be turned. Speech in fact depends on what we understand as writing. The centre depends on the periphery; meaning, the signified, depends on the circulation of signifiers. The speech/writing distinction is therefore not just an oddity, or an example among others of the quirkiness of language, but touches on the core of what it is to claim access to meaning and impinges on metaphysics.

Speech in fact depends on what we understand as writing.

Implications for architecture

These reflections on language resonate with and have inspired certain attitudes to architecture, where architecture is explored as a text, as writing. Another term Derrida uses for proto-writing is arche-writing. The prefixes, proto- and arche-, function to delineate a first, primary, basic, foundational, *proto*typical, *arche*typical condition on which the stem (following the prefix) of the word is founded. The prefix is attached to the de-privileged term in an opposition, as if to elevate its status over some opposing term. It takes little imagination to see the possibilities for play on the word 'architecture': arche-tecture, arche-texture, arch(e)tecture. The word 'architect' derives from the Greek for master builder, *arkhitektonikos*. The *tekton* is a builder or carpenter, a word that also relates to *tekhne*, 'as art'. The words 'technical', 'tectonic', 'text' and 'texture' share a similar root. The emphasis in architecture, according to its etymology at least, falls on tectonics, material configurations. There is nothing here about ideas, cosmos, knowledge, wisdom, meaning, or a medium of transcendence for the human spirit. The architect is the mere craftsman.

In his important book *Republic*, Plato effectively sets up an opposition between the philosopher on the one hand, the lover of wisdom with access to the world of Ideas, and the mere *tekton* on the other. The tradesman (*tekton*) builds copies of the ideas, and is in the subservient position (Plato, 1941, pp. 331–332). Reconstitutions of the word 'architecture' as 'arche-tecture' and its variants attempt a similar revision to that exercised in the elevation of writing over speech and the definition of an arche-writing. In any case Derrida seems to argue for a downgrading of philosophy from a concern with ideas to a vindication of the art and practice of putting words down in writing. This brings philosophy into the practical domain of architecture. In other words, one of the main outcomes of Structuralism and Poststructuralism for architecture is to reassert, or at least to wrestle with, architecture's materiality over its ideologies, to treat architecture and to theorise architecture by considering its groundedness, its textures, plumbing, specificity and its everydayness in social and urban contexts: its potions, poisons, paints and parasites. Another way to look at the implications for architecture is to think of what Structuralism/ Poststructuralism displaces from architectural discourse, or at least how it renders certain concepts problematic and contingent: concepts of authenticity, original meanings, intentions, higher meanings, deeper meanings, fundamentals, authenticity, the essential, the transcendence of architecture, architecture as a medium for expressing the spirit of an age, architecture as an expression of the intentions of the designer, drawings and models as representations of the ideas of the designer, the spirit of place, origins, concepts of genius, objectivity, subjectivity and theory as a foundation for practice. In the next chapter I examine how some of Derrida's thoughts were taken up by architects in the 1980s and 1990s.

one of the main outcomes of Structuralism and

Poststructuralism for architecture is to reassert, or at least to

wrestle with, architecture's materiality over its ideologies, to

treat architecture and to theorise architecture by considering

its groundedness, its textures, plumbing, specificity and its

everydayness in social and urban contexts: its potions, poisons,

paints and parasites.

CHAPTER 4

Derrida on Architecture

In this chapter I address Derrida's encounters with architects, in particular with Peter Eisenman and the project known as *Chora L Works*, an unbuilt park within the Parc de la Villette on the outskirts of Paris (Wigley, 1987; Papadakis *et al.*, 1989; Derrida and Hanel, 1990; Eisenman, 1990; Kipnis, 1991; Soltan, 1991; Patin, 1993; Kipnis and Leeser, 1997; Benjamin, 2000). Derrida's major encounter with architects began in 1984. It is instructive to see what led to this event.

Derrida's first influential book, *On Grammatology*, was published in French in 1967 and appeared in English translation in 1974. Collections of his essays were, however, available in English in the 1960s. Derrida's radical intellectualism seemed to fit the mood of the era augured by the violent protests by students in Paris in 1968, among whom he gained a following. Derrida's thinking had already impacted on the intellectual climate in the United States in 1966 when he presented at a seminal conference, 'Criticism and the Sciences of Man', at Johns Hopkins University in Baltimore (Lamont, 1987, p. 609). Many other French philosophers and theorists with a following in the United States were there, including Roland Barthes, Claude Lévi-Strauss, Jacques Lacan and Paul de Man. According to biographer David Mikics (2010, p. 94), Derrida gave 'one of his most dazzling performances' at this conference, trumping those present with a carefully argued and pointed polemic about the end of Structuralism, with pointed reference to the life's work of Lévi-Strauss, one of the main conference contributors.

According to sociologist Michele Lamont (1987, p. 595), the diffusion of Derrida's work peaked at the start of the 1970s, but we can observe that it did not impact on architectural thinking until the mid-1980s. Architectural theorists came late to engaging with Derrida and Deconstruction. While Derrida's ideas were being disseminated and debated within philosophy and literary studies in the 1970s, architecture was preoccupied with other themes. Primary among them was a kind of scientific rationalism and empiricism, inflected in various ways through design methods, systems theory, cybernetics and nascent computer-aided design studies. Leading figures included Richard Buckminster Fuller and Geoffrey Broadbent. History was also primary as a theoretical force, in particular with leanings towards Historicism, a legacy of Romanticism that implies purpose and progress to world events. According to Historicism, architecture distils the spirit of a time and a people in its buildings. One thinks of the dominance of Sigfried Giedion (1888–1968) and his heirs and detractors. The third force was Phenomenology, a scholarly discourse that drew on the writings of Martin Heidegger that were championed in architecture by Kenneth Frampton and Christian Norberg-Schultz. The fourth theme was Structuralism, examined in the preceding chapters, the major summative architectural text for which appeared in 1969 under the title *Meaning in Architecture* (Jencks and Baird, 1969). Advocates and critics of the style of architecture commonly referred to as Postmodernism drew on the language of Structuralism, particularly its deployment of the concept of the sign and the building as a sign. Robert Venturi and Denise Scott Brown's *Learning from Las Vegas* (Venturi *et al.*, 1993) constitutes one of the most accessible texts pertaining to this theme. As was the case with philosophy, politics and cultural theory in general, Structuralism was also taken forward by neo-Marxists and members and heirs of critical theory and the Frankfurt School, in architecture represented by theorists such as Manfredo Tafuri (Tafuri, 1996).

While Derrida's ideas were being disseminated and debated within philosophy and literary studies in the 1970s, architecture was preoccupied with other themes.

Bernard Tschumi is the architect, educator and theorist most commonly associated with introducing Derrida to architects. Tschumi's compilation of his own essays and excerpts, *Architecture and Disjunction*, was published in 1996 with essays dating back to 1975. The language is Structuralist, or Poststructuralist, invoking concepts of oppositions, ambiguity, disruption, disjunction and disturbance. In these works he cites Jacques Lacan, Georg Batailles and Martin Heidegger, but there is no mention of Jacques Derrida. The online archive of academic articles known as JSTOR provides an easy tool for reckoning trends in academic scholarship. There are negligible numbers of articles in the architecture category that reference Derrida prior to 1980.

This late start is by no means unusual in the slow diffusion of ideas between disciplines, particularly prior to the development of online library resources, e-journals and the Internet. What does it take to encourage the diffusion of a set of ideas into any discipline, and into architecture in particular? We may suppose that architecture is a late-starter in the realms of theory, of whatever complexion, in part as it has such a wide range of issues to contend with: construction, professional practice, design, economics. It is also the case that its modes of diffusion include legitimation via pictorial material, designs, buildings and the endorsement from high-status individuals, particularly famous architects and educators. Not least among the many factors that influence the diffusion of ideas into architecture is the issue of apparent relevance, which in turn is a matter of language and terminology. The architectural theorist Mark Wigley argues convincingly that Derrida's writing was always 'haunted' by architecture, with Derrida's reference to structure, topology and the intruder in the home (Wigley, 1995). Derrida makes reference to formalism and 'spacing' in *Of Grammatology* (1976, pp. 200–201), though these terms have currency in literary studies in any case. Derrida makes fleeting reference to architecture via Kant in an article with Craig Owens published in the journal *October* in 1979. But it seems that architecture was only nascent in Derrida's writing until he started to work with architects. The writing of Derrida's essay entitled 'Chora' (a Greek word commonly translated as 'space') was in progress some time before his meeting with Eisenman, and *chora* became a motif in his interaction with Eisenman.

According to some commentators, the high-profile architecture of the 1980s would no doubt have continued to develop as it did without Derrida, and for much architecture of the time Derrida's writing served as a means of explaining, justifying and contextualising the work of the architectural avant-garde, rather than inspiring or motivating it. The book *Deconstruction: A Student Guide*, presents Deconstruction's success graphically, though the text by Geoffrey Broadbent, while paying homage, seeks to put deconstructive architecture in its place. Broadbent cautions the reader as to the limited scope of Deconstruction, raising the question of whether architecture needs Derrida, bearing in mind that various challenging deconstructive practical and argumentative strategies were already in play among avant-garde architects, such as Venturi, without reference to Derrida's philosophy:

> For quite independently – or so it seems – he [Venturi] and Derrida were thinking on equivalent lines: of 'Both–And' or 'undecidables', of 'transparency' and how undesirable it was. And whilst his approach may seem, and actually is, chaotic, Derrida's 'deconstruction' is at least sustained.
>
> (Broadbent and Glusberg, 1991, p. 64)

Catherine Cooke associates the style of architecture commonly characterised as Deconstruction with Russian Formalism (Cooke, 1989). There were in any case other interesting thinkers already mentioned (Venturi) who challenged the conventions of architecture, and adopted the language of sign, art and culture to do so.

Reflecting further on the slow diffusion of his ideas into architecture, Derrida's work was also difficult to grasp for those uninitiated in philosophy, or who were not so familiar with the protagonists in his critiques. Several lucid texts explaining Derrida's thinking to the uninitiated were key in the diffusion of his ideas within architecture. Notable among these was the book by the Cornell English professor Jonathan Culler called *On Deconstruction: Theory and Criticism after Structuralism*, published in 1982. The first edition makes scant reference to architectural themes, though Culler explains clearly the seductive spatial Derridean problematic of *presence*, as well as the metaphors of trace and graft. These themes are later picked up by Eisenman who references Derrida, via Culler, in his article 'The end of the classical: The end of the beginning, the end

Frank Gehry's House, Santa Monica, California (credit Richard Williams).

Frank Gehry's Dancing House, Prague, Czech Republic.

Berlin Jewish Museum, Daniel Libeskind, Berlin, Germany.

of the end', which appeared in 1984. As far as can be ascertained, this essay by Eisenman was the first written work of note by an architectural theorist that refers to Derrida's writing.

Eisenman was already well-known for a series of articles, books and buildings that explored ideas relating language to architecture. His approach drew on Structuralism, playing on themes of grammar, syntax and meaning. The recently (1984) completed Wexler building at Ohio State University, with its conflicting grid systems, and fragmented historical and contextual references, had been

Memorial to the Murdered Jews of Europe, Peter Eisenman, Berlin, Germany.

hailed as a prime example of the Postmodern in architecture. Eisenman had also completed an acclaimed design for the town square of Cannaregio in Italy in 1978 and a project for the Venice Biennale that he called 'Romeo and Juliet'.

I have already referred to Bernard Tschumi. At about the time Eisenman was finishing his article on the end of classicism, Tschumi was watching the realisation of his major Parc de la Villette project. The park was built on the site of an old abattoir on the outskirts of Paris. The design incorporated a long canal and was overlaid by a formal grid pattern. The intersection of each grid line was marked by the presence of a large steel-frame structure painted bright red. Tschumi referred to these forms as 'follies'.

Tschumi had trained in architecture at the ETH (Eidgenössische Technische Hochschule) in Zurich. His career in the 1970s spanned Paris, London and New York. In the 1970s he followed the writings of the French avant-garde who collected around the journal *Tel Quel*, one of Derrida's main publishing outlets. Roland Barthes was one of Tschumi's main sources, but Tschumi was familiar with Derrida's writing, though his 1981 portfolio book *The Manhattan Transcripts* does not reference Derrida (Kipnis, 1991, p. 60). As Tschumi explains, his Parc de la Villette project was the winning design in an international architectural competition to rehabilitate large areas of Paris. His vision for the park was to bring together artists and writers as well as designers in a cultural exchange:

> **Bringing together various disciplines and establishing crossovers was a key concept of the park, in the same way as in my earlier activity as a teacher at the Architectural Association and at Princeton in the mid-1970s, I would give my students texts by Kafka, Calvino, Hegel, Poe, Joyce and other authors as programs for architectural projects.**
>
> **(Tschumi, 1997, p. 125)**

Tschumi proposed that interdisciplinary teams would design individual gardens within the park, under the general structure of Tschumi's overall point-grid design. Those he encouraged to participate included the philosopher and writer Jean-François Lyotard, one of the leading figures in the definition of Postmodernism (Lyotard, 1986). Lyotard eventually decided not to participate, and not all collaborative projects were brought to completion. Tschumi approached Derrida, who also required some persuasion. According to Tschumi: 'The major questioning of the time, undertaken against the current hegemony of historicist revivals, saw a number of poststructuralist thinkers contributing to architects' conversations, one of them being Jacques Derrida' (1997, p. 125). Apparently, on their meeting, Derrida inquired of Tschumi why architects should be interested in his work since 'deconstruction is anti-form, anti-hierarchy, anti-structure – the opposite of all that architecture stands for' (Tschumi, 1997, p. 125). 'Precisely for this reason', was Tschumi's reply. Tschumi was keen therefore to bring together Peter Eisenman, who was engaged with a range of disciplines and pursued a Formalist approach to architecture, and Derrida as 'the proponent of anti-form'. The architect and the philosopher were to lead a team designing a themed section of the Parc de la Villette. Philosopher met

Parc de la Villette, by Bernard Tschumi.

Parc de la Villette, Panorama of Folly.

theoretician-architect, a potent mix that influenced architectural thinking for a decade.

So the diffusion of Derrida's thinking into architecture did not emerge until this encounter in 1984.[1] Important in the discussion of ideas into architectural discourse is the production of some key large-format books. This production took place in the latter part of the 1980s and into the 1990s. Once Derrida's ideas take hold, much of the scholarship presents as an attempt to assess Derrida's importance for architecture, to critique this importance and more importantly to critique the designs and their architects who purport to be delivering works influenced by Derrida. Deconstruction reproduces itself in architecture through both advocacy and criticism.

Parc de la Villette, Folly.

Deconstruction reproduces itself in architecture through both advocacy and criticism.

Pivotal in this diffusion effect were a series of notes, letters, drawings and articles dating from 1985 (with illustrations dating earlier) that were published as a book called *Chora L Works: Jacques Derrida and Peter Eisenman* (Kipnis and Leeser, 1997), the first part of the title referencing Derrida's interpretation of Plato on the theme of *chora*, understood as space, but as a kind of third space between the material and the immaterial (to be explored in more detail in the chapter that follows). This book was followed in 1988 by an exhibition at New York's Museum of Modern Art featuring the work of Eisenman, Tschumi and Zaha Hadid (Richards, 2008, p. 64). The exhibition in turn gave birth to the book

Deconstruction: Omnibus Volume (Papadakis *et al.*, 1989). A further large-format book appeared in 1991, *Deconstruction: A Student Guide*.

So *Chora L Works* collates key texts introducing Derrida's thinking to architects. The form of the book is distinctive. It has 212 pages, is square in format, measuring 22 cm × 22 cm, and is perforated by eight square cut-out shapes that penetrate from the cover to page 112. There are ten further perforations penetrating from the back cover to page 125. These perforations, just under 1 cm square, follow the two overlaid grid patterns of the eventual design for the park-garden, which is in turn illustrated in plan on the front cover of the book and in the intervening pages. The perforations interrupt the text: one grid is skewed and one is in line with the margins of the book. More than half the book is taken up with textual material that extends to the page margins without columns or paragraph breaks. This densely formatted sans serif text is treated as if a grey texture across the page. The book, its design, the un-annotated park-garden design and the text constitute the tangible outcome of this unbuilt project.

Experimentation with the form and shape of literary, academic and art books is not unusual, and Derrida's book *Glas*, first published in French 1974, presents parallel columns of interweaving text and in different fonts. There is a tendency here in the emergence of such literary and publication conventions to make explicit the reader's complicity in developing sense from the text, and in a way contributing to the role of the reader: the author and reader as *bricoleur*. In the case of *Chora L Works*, the perforations interrupt the text and the reader has to infer what is missing by attending to the immediate context of the surrounding words, arguably a further exercise in making explicit the character of all reading. The form of the book also reflects the proposal to excavate through the ground plane of the site to create a series of receptacles, the major formal elements of the park design.

The drawings give little indication of the scale of the proposed project or its context. The most prominent site plan indicates Venice, rather than Paris, and the description in the text elides the issue of scale with overlays and various conceptual transformations. The initial focus of the project appears to be the middle section of the Parc de la Villette defined by the large circular path.

In making the text difficult to read, the book, and the architectural project, in effect privilege the illustrations and the advocacy of the project above the complex play between advocacy and criticism that the text advances. Some of the articles that are more easily read can be sourced from other publications, such as Jeffrey Kipnis's article which also appeared in the journal *Assemblage*. The form of the book also appears as an attempt to obscure the disagreements evident in the text. Kipnis, editor of the volume and associate of Eisenman, notes pointedly that Eisenman and Derrida appeared to be at cross-purposes in the architectural project, a relationship marked by 'defensiveness, duplicity, and conflict', under the guise of an intimate friendship (1991, p. 33). The *Deconstruction: Omnibus Edition*, while cashing in on the topic of the decade, contains similarly cautioning criticism by Charles Jencks and others:

> **And here is the real contradiction in Deconstruction: in spite of the claims to pluralism, *différance*, 'a war on totality' and defence of 'otherness', this hermetic work is often monist, elitist, intolerant and conveys a 'sameness'. Perhaps, in architecture, this is a result of staring into the Void for too long: it has resulted in a private religious language of self-denial. Because of such suppressions and contradictions one could argue that a real Deconstructionist architecture of variety and humour has yet to exist.**
>
> (Jencks, 1989, p. 131)

The circulation of thinking about Deconstruction in architecture persisted, in spite of, or perhaps because of, such criticisms.

Chora L Works

A detailed reading of the various transcripts and essays in the joint volume by Kipnis, Eisenman and Derrida is revealing of Derrida's encounter with architecture. *Chora L Works* begins with the edited transcript of the initial design meeting on 17 September 1885 in New York between Derrida, Eisenman and others, with substantial input from the editor Jeffrey Kipnis. In this first transcribed meeting, Derrida expresses his interest in the concept of *chora*, identified by Plato in *Timaeus*. Under Derrida's reading, *chora* constitutes a third space between (i) the realm of ideas, that distant but invisible solid realm in which reside the eternal and unchanging forms and ideals, and (ii) the sensible world that we occupy in the here and now: the imperfect world of human experience that contains only so many imperfect copies of the ideas. *Chora*, as a third, contradictory entity of containment, precedes the other two and is irreducible to them:

> **Since it is absolutely blank, everything that is printed on it is automatically effaced. It remains foreign to the imprint it receives.... Everything inscribed in it erases itself immediately, while remaining in it. It is thus an impossible surface – it is not even a surface, because it has no depth.**
>
> **(Kipnis and Leeser, 1997, p. 10)**

As the *chora* concept is explained at their meeting, Eisenman sees the problematic of *chora* as the outline of a possible program and asks, 'Now are we going to try physically to embody this program?' Derrida retorts, 'That would be the height of anthropocentrism' (Kipnis and Leeser, 1997, p. 10), i.e. an attempt to ground reason in the sovereignty of humankind, a variant of metaphysics, an unregenerate belief in certainties. Eisenman sees here the possibility of constructing 'the absence of *chora*.... The presence of the absence of *chora*' (Kipnis and Leeser, 1997, p. 10). After further discussion, including of Eisenman's previous projects, they agree to meet again having read more of each other's work.

An English translation of Derrida's essay 'Chora' constitutes the second chapter of the book. This perforated (physically), abstrusely formatted and therefore difficult to read essay seems to be the only English version in print. Derrida had already commenced the essay before he met with Eisenman, and it was completed over the course of their interaction. In the essay Derrida makes reference to Plato's book *Timaeus*, where Plato describes the problematic of the origins of the elements: earth, air, fire and water. There are two forms of reality: the intelligible and unchanging model, and the changing copy of it, able to be apprehended by the senses (Plato, 1965). There are thus two spaces, places, models, realms: the Intelligible and the Sensible. This is the underlying opposition of Platonic thought. But in part 16 of *Timaeus* Plato introduces this third place as the origin of both the intelligible and the sensible. This is the 'receptacle of becoming' (Plato, 1965, p. 67). Plato later in *Timaeus* deploys the Greek word *chora* (space) to designate it. Plato maintains that this 'third form' is complex and obscure. It is 'the nurse of all becoming and change'. (I elaborate on these explanations in the next chapter.)

The third section of *Chora L Works* is an edited transcript, dated 8 November 1985, of the second design meeting, held in Paris. The assembled team wrestle with *chora* as a motivation for their project. Eisenman suggests: 'One possibility is to use sand and water – sand for writing, water for erasing.... There should also be a sense of dislocation' (Kipnis and Leeser, 1997, p. 34). Derrida seems to like Eisenman's precedence of a house with a room that you can look into but never enter as a good analogy for *chora*. Then follows a discussion of Freud's use of the mystic writing pad as a metaphor for the unconscious, the paradoxical nature of *chora*, the idea of a park that induces walking backwards, de-training users of the park from thinking in terms of representation, and the denigration of the idea of an origin. They also discuss their intention to create a book out of the project, and the pragmatic resolve to bring design drawings to the next meeting. Eisenman introduces the idea of dividing the site into a quarry, a palimpsest and a labyrinth. Derrida says of the latter that this plan suggests hope in an exit, which does not really accord with the concept of *chora*. They discuss the practicality, and impracticality, of providing opportunities for users of the park to transfer imprints from one part to another. They discuss the medium of clay paste and also video and film. Derrida is concerned about the safety of such operations if carried out by the public.

The fourth transcribed meeting is held in New York. The conversation begins with a complaint that another architect (Alain Pelissier, who was present at their second recorded meeting) has already been commissioned to put something in the middle of their site. There seemed to be some kind of resolution reached before the meeting involving taking over a different part of the La Villette site. The conversation moves to the matter of *chora* and the difficulties in relating it to the project. Plato genders *chora* as feminine. *Chora* is a receptacle; everything is inscribed on it, but it remains virginal. Derrida asserts that the receptacle is only a metaphor. Derrida says: 'So we have only the use of bad metaphors; indeed the concept of metaphor itself is "bad"; it has no pertinance ... But we cannot avoid metaphors ... just as we cannot avoid buildings' (Kipnis and Leeser, 1997, p. 70). Eisenman is also keen to show the connections between Tschumi's design for the Parc de la Villette and Eisenman's own unbuilt but widely disseminated Cannaregio project, which was also intended for an old abattoir site. The projects are similar in their use of the point grid, though Eisenman wants to assert 'no claim to prior authorship' (Kipnis and Leeser, 1997, p. 72). The quarry theme is raised: there is a sense in which ideas are quarried from various projects. The conversation deviates to an account of how Eisenman and Derrida were introduced by Tschumi, and several coincidental events in terms of their various written and designed works. They discuss the title of their project, which is to be 'Choral Works'. 'Great', declares Eisenman, 'now we have everything – we have you, me, a story and a title.' To which Derrida retorts, 'It remains to do the work' (Kipnis and Leeser, 1997, pp. 72–73). There is talk of the money they are getting for the project, and Derrida introduces the French word *maintenant*, translated into English as 'now', but inflected by Derrida as the concept of 'maintaining the dislocation, maintaining the difference' (Kipnis and Leeser, 1997, p. 73). This theme is elaborated in a further article not included in the book (Derrida, 1986).

The fifth meeting is held in New Haven, Connecticut. Eisenman and his associate Thomas Leeser explain their proposals for the site through a series of axonometric drawings. The design makes reference, through shapes and layerings, to Eisenman's earlier Cannaregio scheme, his Venice Biennale project ('Romeo and Juliet') and Tschumi's Parc de la Villette design. But the temporal (causal) aspect is inverted: 'we have Venice as a future for Bernard's project and La Villette as the present for Peter's Cannaregio scheme' (Kipnis and Leeser, 1997, p. 77). The temporal aspect is manifested in terms of the relationships between solids and voids across the site. According to Leeser: 'Everything that is underground, negative form, has a reading as a receptacle, either past or present. It depends on how deep it goes into the ground' (Kipnis and Leeser, 1997, p. 78). They agree that a further element is needed that 'ruptures the fabric' (Kipnis and Leeser, 1997, p. 90), something like a sudden unexplainable slab of stainless steel, like the slab in *2001: A Space Odyssey*, but probably on the horizontal plane. They agree that Derrida will invent this heterogeneous element and its positioning on the site before they next meet.

Subsequently, on his flight back to Paris, Derrida generates a drawing of an object derived from his reading of Plato's *Timaeus*. It has the rough outline of a grand piano in plan, and is harp-like, unusable as an instrument as the strings are configured as a grid. It appears at an angle on the page as if resting one corner on a ground line. His handwritten note (appearing later in the book) refers to the object as a lyre, a screen, a sieve, a riddle, a work of braided rope, and a filter. He refers to scalings, its construction in metal, with gold:

> planted oblique to the sun, neither vertical nor horizontal, a solid frame resembling, at the same time, a framework (loom), a sieve, or a grille (grid), and also a stringed musical instrument (piano, harp, lyre): string, stringed instrument, vocal chords, etc.... telescope, or photographic revealer, a machine, fallen from the sky, after having photographed ... it will make a sign (signify?) to the concert and the multiple chorale, the *chora* of Choral Works.
>
> (Kipnis and Leeser, 1997, p. 185)

Many of the elements he describes are present, or suggested, in Plato's *Timaeus*.

The section of the book following the fifth transcript presents copies of correspondence between Tschumi and Eisenman, where Tschumi takes exception to the claim, as apparently reported in the press, that Eisenman asserts La Villette was derived from Eisenman's Cannaregio design. Eisenman replies with the claim that he was misreported, along with an apology that he was not more attentive to the press copy when it was sent to him for approval.

The sixth meeting is held in New York. The design as it develops involves holes and voids configured with walls, embankments and battlements involving pre-rusted Cor-ten steel and marble (onyx). The team think that people would not be permitted to enter the space, but look down onto it. If there is to be access then the holes in the ground plane could be covered with glass. Perhaps handrails are needed, and a moat. Derrida does not like the idea of keeping people out, i.e. turning the place into an object, 'worse, a sacred object' (Kipnis and Leeser, 1997, p. 90). Various solutions are proposed, including submerging the whole construction under water, with parts projecting above the water level. The team seem to settle on elaborate subterranean access points, that 'allow the public to enter the underneath, where you would see the inverse of everything: the surface as a ceiling and all the articulations, the solids and the voids of the surface, in inverse' (Kipnis and Leeser, 1997, p. 91). Eisenman sees this solution as a return to Derrida's theme of *chora*. They then proceed to explain the entire scheme and the process to a newly arrived visitor to the group, Frank Gehry, whose comments, if there are any, are not reported in the text. The triumphant vein continues with reflections on the relationship between the philosopher, Derrida, and the architect, Eisenman. The project was apparently only able to reach this level of resolution when the philosopher and the architect were able to confront each other with their differences. At this point Kipnis interjects with a criticism of Derrida's naivety in his choice of the sieve or lyre as a representative symbol of his formal contribution to the project, and to Eisenman's nostalgia for form. Eisenman admits to being in awe of Derrida and to putting himself in a 'lesser position' in relation to the great philosopher. The responses of Derrida, who eschews such psychologising (Mikics, 2010), give assent, but are succinct.

This section of the book is followed by a more fulsome reflection by Derrida on the encounter, the naming of the project and his justification for contributing the lyre-sieve motif, including the pun between lyre and liar. The essay is called 'Why Peter Eisenman writes such good books', a corruption of a title used by Friedrich Nietzsche ('Why I write such good books'). Derrida manages to connect each of Eisenman's references to Eisenman's own writings and designs that have arisen in the course of their discussions through a series of puns, including

Peter Eisenman's name: his first name related to stone (Peter) and his surname (Eisenman) to iron. The chapter contains a faintly veiled slight on Eisenman's work:

> Nevertheless, I tell you the truth. It is the truth of this man of iron, determined to break with the anthropocentric scale, with 'man the measure of all things': he writes such good books! I swear it to you! This is what all liars say; they would not be lying if they did not say they were telling the truth.
>
> (Kipnis and Leeser, 1997, p. 100)

The final transcript in the book relates a discussion at Cooper Union architecture school, New York, between Derrida, Eisenman and Kipnis, in front of an audience. The majority of the transcript is devoted to Derrida, who begins by reflecting on how Deconstruction differs from philosophy, and on the sacred origins of architecture, which is to say its metaphysical basis. Here and elsewhere he alludes to areas to which Deconstruction applies, but that are neglected by architecture, at least as Derrida presents it:

> And what is at stake in architecture is, of course, not only metaphysics, religion in its discursive form, but also politics, the teaching institutions, the economy, the culture. The negotiations between an architect such as Peter and all the powers which prevent you from building, this negotiation is precisely the place where deconstruction as architecture, or as an architecture, could take place.
>
> (Kipnis and Leeser, 1997, p. 106)

Derrida repeats an assertion he made in several discussions and interviews: 'you cannot say that *chora* is architecture or a new space for architecture' (Kipnis and Leeser, 1997, p. 109). Contrary to the interpretation Eisenman and other architects seem to put on the concept of *chora*, it is not a void. Neither is it a thing. The only concession Derrida seems to offer to this apparent misconception is that 'Perhaps architecture is the most powerful attempt just to forget space, forget *chora*' (Kipnis and Leeser, 1997, p. 109). Later in the public discussion, Eisenman challenges Derrida on his apparently self-deprecating claim to incompetence in architecture: 'We say we cannot talk to you because [we] are not philosophers and you say I cannot talk to you because you are not an architect' (Kipnis and Leeser, 1997, p. 110). An audience member asks how Derrida would name the collaboration. Derrida replies, 'It is certainly not a collaboration. It is even less an exchange. How would you call it, Peter?' 'An adhesion', replies Eisenman. Derrida adds: 'It is a double parasitic laziness' (Kipnis and Leeser, 1997, p. 111).

The transcripts end at this half-way point in the book, and there is temporary respite from the perforations. There is a deliberately misplaced frontispiece, publisher's front matter, the table of contents, illustration credits and a one-page introduction by Bernard Tschumi. Then follows a further series of (perforated) articles. The first by Eisenman leads towards a guarded identification of Derrida, or at least their interaction, with the mythic trickster function as outlined by the psychologist Karl Jung, and here Eisenman adds to 'parasitic laziness' the coda 'separate tricks' (Kipnis and Leeser, 1997, p. 136).

Then follows a detailed analysis of the preceding essays and transcripts by Jeffrey Kipnis, the editor of the book and associate of Eisenman, entitled 'Twisting the separatrix'. As well as playing on 'separate tricks', the separatrix is the oblique stroke, or forward slash, that is commonly used to separate the two elements of an opposition: ornament/structure, signifier/signified, S/s, raw/cooked, and/or. As I indicated in Chapter 2 it is an obvious occurrence in Structuralism and in Derrida's writing. In this insightful essay, Kipnis quotes a comment from Eisenman from a conference in Chicago that is not in the transcripts:

> And so when I made the first crack at the project we were doing together – a public garden in Paris – he said things to me that filled me with horror: 'How can it be a garden without plants?' 'Where are the trees?' 'Where are the benches for people to sit on?' This is what philosophers want, they want to know where the benches are.
>
> (I reference the edition of the paper (which is easier to read)
> that appeared in *Assemblage* (Kipnis, 1991, p. 36))

Kipnis affirms that the encounter with Derrida did not produce anything that Eisenman would not have done anyway, or at least:

> it cannot be said that the garden evidences any significant directional change for Eisenman that can be expressly attributed to Derrida's participation. Eisenman prevented that from happening, as we shall see, though he and Derrida agreed that it must happen.
>
> (Kipnis, 1991, p. 36)

Kipnis identifies from the transcripts several of Derrida's design propositions, of whatever merit, barely acknowledged by Eisenman: printing and erasure; simplicity; not a masterwork; uses earth, air, fire and water; employs light and sound through electronic devices; not circular or totalising. It seems that Derrida's attempt to upset the totalising aspect of the project by inserting an unrelated, heterogeneous element (the lyre-sieve), was tacitly accepted, but when the drawing of Derrida's object arrived it was duly ignored, or at least marginalised as a component in the project.

when the drawing of Derrida's object arrived it was duly

ignored, or at least marginalised as a component in the

project.

Derrida's misgivings about the collaboration are given further vent in his 'Letter to Eisenman', an audio recording he dispatched to a conference in Irvine, California, at which Eisenman was present, but which Derrida was unable to attend. Derrida sees Eisenman as an unrepentant metaphysician, perhaps who is not even wrestling with the dilemmas Derrida presents to him: '*chora* is neither the void, as you suggest sometimes, nor absence, nor invisibility, nor certainly the contrary from which there are, and this is what interests me, a large number of consequences' (I refer here to the reprint in *Assemblage* (Derrida and Hanel, 1990, p. 8)). Derrida's grievance about the project is clear: 'If I had come [to the conference], I would have spoken perhaps of my own displacement in the course of "choral work" ' (Derrida and Hanel, 1990, p. 8). Among other challenges, Derrida invites Eisenman to reflect on other matters pertinent to architecture: poverty, social housing and homelessness.

Derrida asserts similarly in the Afterword to the book, a transcript of an interview by Jeffrey Kipnis:

> What makes architectural deconstruction more affirmative, consequential and effective than deconstruction in discourse is that it encounters and must attempt to overcome the most effective resistances – cultural, political, social, economic, financial, material and architectural.... Thus architecture, and for similar reasons the law, are the ultimate tests of deconstruction.
>
> (Kipnis, 1991, p. 167)

Derrida recalls from the transcripts that it was he who posed the questions of resistance, about technical possibility, economics and safety. Kipnis puts to Derrida the proposition that Derrida's ideas were largely ignored by Eisenman. Derrida also talks about authorship, and dismisses the suggestion that Deconstruction might constitute a style of architecture:

Derrida recalls from the transcripts that it was he who posed the questions of resistance, about technical possibility, economics and safety.

> Here's what must be done beyond the negative motifs of architectural deconstruction which have so far been explored. The deconstruction of architecture in the broader sense will yield an architecture which is no longer a closed, identifiable and specific field. Consequently, architecture must be confronted as being more than building design or buildings. It must be explored as having to do with relationships, including urbanism, of course, but moving beyond what one calls 'culture' in general.
>
> (Kipnis and Leeser, 1997, p. 170)

Derrida affirms that 'there will be no objects that one can identify as deconstructive' (Kipnis and Leeser, 1997, p. 171). The closing sections of the book include Eisenman's reply to Derrida's letter, concluding: 'In the end, my architecture cannot be what it should be, but only what it can be' (Kipnis and Leeser, 1997, p. 189).

The book *Chora L Works* contains many more words than I have alluded to here and a complexity of themes and discussions that I have just skated over, but are given fuller treatment in Kipnis's essay in the book. It is clear from the transcripts that personality played a role in the collaboration/adhesion, as did cultural differences and differences in intellectual tradition. The mutual parasitism of which Derrida and Eisenman speak pertains not only to design, but reputation, status, legitimation, disciplinary territories and 'authorial investment' (or 'signing a work') (Kipnis and Leeser, 1997, p. 168). In his interview by Kipnis, Derrida asserts: 'If my participation in this project was merely as a petty, legitimizing force in the field of architecture, I would escape immediately' (Kipnis and Leeser, 1997, p. 170).

The architecture described in *Chora L Works*, and the approach to architecture it exposes, fits the charge advanced by many that architecture, or at least this variant of it, only too readily becomes a self-referential discipline guarded against the public. For Eisenman, the design of the park seems motivated by a series of cross-references to a particular circuit of work, built and unbuilt. The work arguably borrows from ideas about 'intertextuality', but the 'texts' to which it refers are those of a very particular circuit, other projects by the author. How does the proposed park intersect with the texts of the putative users of the site? Even conceding that the idea of the public and the user might be implicit rather than explicit in the work of an architect, one has to search hard for any concept, even tacit, of a public, polis, desire or demographic, let alone concepts of participative design, the identification of needs and the acknowledgement of regulation and planning constraints. Derrida seems alert to issues (e.g. health and safety) beyond Eisenman's apparent formalism and less intent on making an architectural statement independent of the human users of the park. With its cross-referencing and critical self-awareness, the book *Chora L Works* itself demonstrates a penchant for intertextuality, but the book is not after all an environment for having a picnic or kicking a football around.

architecture, or at least this variant of it, only too readily becomes a self-referential discipline guarded against the public

If ascertaining user needs appears too functionalist for the French intellectual and Eisenman's architecture then incorporation of the idea of *walking* is not. Think of the *flâneur*, Walter Benjamin's *Arcades Project*, Louis Aragon's *Paris Peasant* and Andre Breton's narrative excursions into the flea markets of Paris (Breton, 1960; Aragon, 1994; Benjamin, 2000). There is no reference in the architectural encounters of *Chora L Works* with Deconstruction to the urban theorist Jean-François Augoyard in his important book *Step by Step: Everyday Walks in a French Urban Housing Project*. This book was published in French in 1979 and references Derrida's *Of Grammatology* on the subject of difference (Augoyard, 2007, p. 105). Augoyard's book is about everyday walking practices, treating walking much as one might talk about language, involving expression and appropriation, understood as the play of small differences and discriminations in the walking practices of individuals and groups as related through their narratives, which conform rarely to the idealised models of master

Central area of the Parc de la Villette, the initial site of Eisenman's project.

planners and architects. Walking is a kind of textual production. This kind of micro-study of actual residents and users of spaces is a long way from Eisenman's design, where people appear as an afterthought, to be excluded or moved underground. Derrida does refer to walking in relation to the Parc de la Villette in his approving essay about Tschumi's work (Derrida, 1986, p. 331), but the theme eludes his project with Eisenman. Augoyard's study was in turn a motivator for Michel de Certeau's *The Practice of Everyday Life*, which appeared in English translation in 1984, with its sections on spatial practices, 'walking in the city', and with reference to Derrida and 'walking rhetorics' (de Certeau, 1984, p. 100).

Derrida's encounter with architects might have been orchestrated differently, e.g. into a student project for the park of La Villette: a collaboration of many, with not just a single outcome but a multiplicity of projects, the kinds of cross-media exercises elucidated in *The Manhattan Transcripts* led by Bernard Tschumi. I mention these sources of urban and architectural theory as they are known in the French context, and predate, or are contemporaneous with, Derrida's excursion into architecture. They are arguably more responsive to Derrida's thinking.

Derrida's encounter with architects might have been orchestrated differently

Subsequent to the *Chora L Works* project, Derrida wrote his essay on Tschumi's Parc de la Villette. He elaborates on Tschumi's claim that the buildings on the site are without purpose, as follies, which connect with madness. The essay is approving, and engages with the features of the park and with what Tschumi has written about it. In the process Derrida articulates what he would expect from Deconstruction in architecture. He outlines four main grid points for architecture, each of which has to be unsettled in any deconstructive treatment of architecture. In other words, so much supposed Deconstruction in architecture is ineffective as Deconstruction unless it tackles these four assumed foundations of architecture. As referenced in the Prologue of this book, the first is the primary importance accorded in the architectural tradition to home, dwelling and hearth. The second is the nostalgia within modern architecture for an origin, a set of primary principles, an ordering, including deference to the sacred origins of architecture. The third foundation is that architecture is heading somewhere, to betterment, improvement and the service of humankind. The fourth foundation is an adherence to concepts of the fine arts, i.e. the pursuit of beauty, harmony and completeness. These foundations are not exclusive to architecture, but architecture gives them the most obvious and tangible expression, through its monumental materiality and the persistence of buildings, through which these cultural foundations are preserved, transferred and resist deconstruction. For Derrida these tangible factors conspire to render 'architecture as the last fortress of metaphysics': 'Any consequent deconstruction would be negligible if it did not take account of this resistance and this transference' (Derrida, 1986, p. 328). It seems at first that Tschumi's follies in the Parc de la Villette succeed in destabilising meaning: 'They put in question, dislocate, destabilize or deconstruct the edifice of this configuration', and there is a madness in this move. But the follies simply 'maintain, renew and reinscribe architecture' (Derrida, 1986, p. 328). They 'are anything but anarchic chaos' (Derrida, 1986, p. 329). The best that the park offers in terms of deconstruction is in anticipation of the architecture to come. The red follies are like dice, and the dice have been cast.

Note

1   For the bibliometrically inclined, it is worth noting that the proportion of articles from journals related to architecture and the history of architecture and that referenced Derrida peaked in the 1990s, with close to 2.8 per cent of architecture articles referring to Derrida. As a comparison, there is the same peak for the mention of Wittgenstein and for Heidegger, though with fewer numbers. An analysis of Derrida-related articles in the fields of literary theory and philosophy, Derrida's home territories, show a flatter trajectory. In other words they started earlier.

CHAPTER 5

Other Spaces

On the one hand, architecture deals in the configuration of spaces by the expert assembly of materials. Such functional assemblies for Le Corbusier constitute 'the masterly, correct and magnificent play of masses brought together in light' (Corbusier, 1931, p. 29). Architects define, order and build spaces. On the other hand, there seem to be spaces that lie outside the tangible, material and buildable that are of no less interest to architects. The advent of computerisation has made architects even more aware of such 'other spaces'. The enthusiasm for cyberspace in the 1990s fuelled the fantasy of fully immersive environments that seem in so many ways to exhibit the properties of the spaces we ordinarily inhabit, but exist only as data in computer memory and networks. In a book *Technoromanticism* (1999) I examined the legacies that promoted cyberspace and the speculations advanced by many enthusiasts that digital networks augur a new future in which human beings become absorbed into a great mind-meld, a new container of everything, the fusion of information, knowledge, time, space and identity. In that book I argued that this cyberspace dream (or nightmare) alludes to Platonic idealism, or at least it presents a post-industrial-age, highly technologised, neo-romantic idealism. Cyberspace is an attempt to create and grasp the immaterial in architecture.

Before examining Derrida's interpretation of Plato on the subject of other spaces, it is worth reviewing a typology of such spaces, worlds or realms, i.e. spaces outside those that get built of stone, metal, glass and wood, including those that inspire cyberspace discourses. The Platonic model provides the most coherent early understanding of 'other' spaces. In *Timaeus* and *Republic* Plato describes the world that is occupied by ideas (Plato, 1941, 1965). These ideas are the unchanging universals: perfect spheres, triangles and other forms, but also perfect goodness, justice, virtue and intelligence. We don't see these ideas, but apprehend their existence by reason. Under various religious traditions this timeless realm is the home of deity, spirit and soul. The second realm to which Plato refers is the world around us as perceived by the senses. It is a faltering copy of the world of ideas. Here triangles are not perfectly formed, leaders make imperfect laws and the most beautiful things have flaws. The world of ideas is referred to as the Intelligible, as it is best understood through the intellect, that is, by thought and reason. The world around us is the Sensible, as it is best apprehended through the senses of vision, hearing, touch and so on.

Plato's characterisation that the Intelligible realm is somehow 'more real' than the Sensible is an early example of the inversion of an assumed polarity. Plato presents an inversion of a commonsense understanding of the relationship between the visible and the invisible. Whereas the Greek literature of Homer alluded to the intangible world of spirits as somewhere vague and ephemeral, Plato describes such other spaces as more real than what we are aware of in the everyday world. In describing this inversion, philosopher Hannah Arendt says of Plato's account: 'the soul is not the shadow of the body, but the body the shadow of the soul' (Arendt, 1958, p. 292). By this account, Plato was putting forward a proposition that was radical in its day.

In his book *Republic*, Plato describes his understanding of the two realms or worlds through the spatial metaphor of the cave (Plato, 1941). We are like prisoners trapped in a cave, who see the reality of the world outside only as shadows in the flickering firelight. Another metaphor Plato uses to account for the relationship between the Intelligible and the Sensible is the concept of imprint. The perfect forms resident in the Intelligible realm get imprinted on the materiality of the Sensible world, as the insignia on a king's ring is imprinted into clay or wax. So what we see around us are so many impressions of a higher perfection that are planted, implanted, impressed into the world. This imprinting process applies to the physical geometries of architecture, which are mere copies of divine geometries. The social, political and everyday behaviours of communities and individuals, to a greater or lesser degree, also bear the imprint of perfect goodness, virtue and wisdom.

The Platonic concept of the universe so divided into the Intelligible and the Sensible recurs throughout history, with its advocates and detractors. Much of the dissent to this aspect of Platonism centres on his student Aristotle, who is often marshalled in advocacy of a more pragmatic, empirical view of the world and human understanding (Aristotle, 1976). In the sphere of human morals and ethics there may well be a higher, principled wisdom to which citizens must connect, namely *sophia*, but the pivotal virtue is *phronesis*, the wisdom acquired by experience and through practical application. In contrast to Plato there is a worldly reality to Aristotle's philosophy that provided the putative inspiration for empirical science, with its emphasis on experimentation and observing the world as it presents itself rather than through ideal abstractions. Twentieth-century Pragmatism also traces itself back to Aristotle. For Aristotle the home of the citizen provides the model for society: the practical relationships between householders in the management of their estate. Though indebted to Plato, Aristotle's philosophy emphasises the day-to-day and the practical.

Vitruvius's account of the seeds of architecture in concepts of firmness, commodity and delight similarly speaks more of practicality than of divine geometries (Vitruvius, 1960). Vitruvius wrote his great advocacy for architecture at the time of the Emperor Augustus, and, in keeping with the philosophy of Rome, was less the Platonist or Aristotelian than a Stoic (McEwen, 2003). Stoicism was a powerful philosophical and social movement. It lacked the literary genius of a Plato or an Aristotle, but presents as a strong undercurrent in the development of human thought, influencing such thinkers as the founder of modern economics, Adam Smith (Smith, 1984). Smith emphasised the moral imperative that society should accept the inequalities that might befall any individual in a competitive free-market, as everything is interconnected and good emerges from the performance of the whole. Gilles Deleuze's abundant use of biological and geological metaphors accounting for interconnections, ruptures and disruptions in world systems is often attributed to Stoicism (Deleuze and Guattari, 1988; Sellars, 1999). Stoicism presented a wholly material view of the universe. Any notion of a divinity is attributed to the summation of all things, which are ultimately interconnected. The transcendently other is simply the total of everything, the unity of all things.

Stoicism also finds expression in romantic, populist literature and film. Think of James Cameron's immersive 3D film *Avatar* (2009), with its technologised notion of interconnected living matter and other neo-primitivist myths.

Utopias also feature prominently in this typology of other spaces, as well as dystopias and fantasy spaces, each of which has received treatment from cultural theorists (Jameson, 2005). The discourse of 'other spaces' exposes a range of interesting oppositions: the immaterial and the material, intelligible and sensible, the whole and the parts, utopia and dystopia, real and virtual, real and even more real.

As we saw in the previous chapter, in *Timaeus*, Plato reveals a further 'other space'. This is the *chora*, to which Derrida refers. Plato describes this third realm:

> We must start our new description of the universe by making a fuller subdivision than we did before; we then distinguished two forms of reality – we must now add a third. Two were enough at an earlier stage, when we postulated on the one hand an intelligible and unchanging model and on the other a visible and changing copy of it. We did not distinguish a third form, considering two would be enough; but now the argument compels us to try to describe in words a form that is difficult and obscure. What must we suppose its powers and nature to be? In general terms, it is the receptacle and, as it were, the nurse of all becoming and change.
>
> (Plato, 1965, p. 67, § 16)

Why does Plato need to introduce this third realm, the receptacle, the nurse of all becoming, in *Timaeus*? *Timaeus* is a book about the origin of the universe, an attempt at a unified story about the primitive elements (earth, air, fire and water), geometry and an understanding of human physiology and psychology. Plato identifies a logical inconsistency in his own concept of the bifurcated universe: the Intelligible and the Sensible. The origin of the forms is happily grounded in the Intelligible realm, but where does the 'clay', the formless matter that receives the forms, come from? Presumably it cannot emanate from the Intelligible realm, as that would imply the Intelligible is somehow incomplete, that it contains entities that change. In fact, Plato asserts that the 'clay' is of necessity unchanging. Transforming clay into different shapes does not change the nature of the clay.

> **It can always be called the same because it never alters its characteristics. For it continues to receive all things, and never itself takes a permanent impress from any of the things that enter it; it is a kind of neutral plastic material on which changing impressions are stamped by the things that enter it, making it appear different at different times.**
>
> **(Plato, 1965, p. 69, § 18)**

So the receptacle, the nurse of becoming and change, is like clay: 'the things which pass in and out of it are copies of the eternal realities, whose form they take in a wonderful way that is hard to describe' (Plato, 1965, p. 69, § 18).

Plato then introduces the metaphor of birth to account for the character of this malleable receptacle. The receptacle is the mother; and the formal, Intelligible model whose imprint it receives is the father. Clearly the receptacle cannot be made up, like matter, of the primitive elements (earth, air, fire and water): 'we shall not be wrong if we describe it as invisible and formless, all-embracing, possessed in a most puzzling way of intelligibility, yet very hard to grasp' (Plato, 1965, p. 70, § 18). The Ancient Greek word Plato uses for this third realm is *hypodoche* (ὑποδοχή), which translators render as 'receptacle'.

A few pages on in his account of the origin of the universe, Plato introduces the term *chora* (χώρα) to label this third realm. *Chora* is commonly translated as 'space' in traditional translations of *Timaeus* (Taylor, 1928, p. 342). In fact, some commentators treat Plato's explanation here as describing the evolution of space as conventionally understood, as if the space of extension, the container of the things of the world, emerged from the receptacle of being (Plato, 1888, p. 45). *Chora* was a word in common usage, as in current Greek language, and also connotes place, location, site, region and country.

Philosophers of science Luc Brisson and Walter Meierstein think of *chora* not as space but as 'spatial medium', 'that in which' and 'that from which' the sensible world is made' (1995, pp. 22, 23). So *chora* is not simply space, but something that is chronologically and logically prior to it. *Chora* has peculiar characteristics. According to Plato:

> space [*chora*] which is eternal and indestructible, which provides a position for everything that comes to be, and which is apprehended without the senses by a sort of spurious reasoning and so is hard to believe in – we look at it indeed in a kind of dream and say that everything that exists must be somewhere and occupy some space [*chora*], and that what is nowhere on heaven or earth is nothing at all.
>
> (Plato, 1965, p. 72, § 20)

For 'spurious reasoning' other translators insert 'bastard reasoning' (Taylor, 1928, p. 342), implying the union between a citizen and an alien, where the legitimacy of their offspring cannot be established (Sallis, 1999, p. 120). *Chora* has this hybrid, illegitimate character, as does the reasoning required to apprehend it.

Plato also introduces the idea of the kind of chaos from which the universe emerged. Here he presents the idea of the sieve or winnowing basket in which elements get combined, sifted, settled and remaindered, which provided the inspiration for Derrida's contribution to Eisenman's *Chora L Works* project outlined in the previous chapter. Several concepts cluster around the *chora*: space, place, chaos, matrix, receptacle, birth, complexity, contradiction, remainder and inexpressibility.

The identification of the *chora* in Plato's universe neatly fits Derrida's Deconstructive formula of identifying a problem or contradiction within an opposition, in this case the bipolar construction of the universe in terms of two realities: the Intelligible (invisible) and the Sensible (visible), implying an obvious priority to the Intelligible, whence come the forms. But endemic to Plato's priority is the concept of something that precedes either, namely the *chora*, a proto-reality. One way to understand Derrida's difficult essay on the *chora* is to see the essay as a polemic asserting the difficulty and problematic imbued in this putative origin. Of the *chora*, Derrida says: 'One cannot even say of it that it is *neither* this *nor* that or that it is *both* this *and* that' (1997, p. 15). For Derrida this paradoxical characteristic of *chora* constitutes a multiple 'oscillation between two poles' (1997, p. 15). *Chora* is an appropriate entity for Derrida to tackle. It involves Plato's admission that this basic and primordial entity, *chora*, requires a spurious, hybridised, illegitimate kind of reasoning, the establishment of a foundational notion that in the same breath denies the possibility of a foundation; the conflation of a materially existing kind of space and its ungraspable properties with a difficult, linguistically based logic.

Needless to say, the account of *chora* I have given here is an attempt at setting the context for Derrida's polemical essay. He attempts no such ordered contextualising in the essay, assuming the reader is already familiar with the legacy of *chora*, or at least with *Timaeus*. Derrida provides no particular concessions for the architectural reader or collaborator. It is salutary for architects to know of the problematic of space, but Derrida provides no suggestion of what an architect might do with this information. The architectural philosopher Andrew Benjamin concurs:

> **The only possibility of a productive link between the presentation of khora [or *chora*] within the dialogue [*Timaeus*] and the activity of architecture is if the analogy were between the dialogue itself [*Timaeus*] and the architectural object. And yet even this analogy will not work.**
>
> **(2000, p. 22)**

The concept clearly failed as well in Derrida's project with Eisenman. Some further work is needed to bring the concept of *chora* home to architecture.

Crossing the line

Derrida's identification of a multiple 'oscillation between two poles' brings to mind the characterisation of another 'other space' as presented by the philosopher Immanuel Kant (1724–1804), as the realm of the sublime. The sublime is that which escapes the reflective observer's capacity to imagine or describe: the extent of the constellations, the size of an atom, pure transcendence, ceasing to be, the terrors of nature, the receptacle of being. For Kant, the response to the beautiful in nature is calm contemplation, but in consideration of the sublime, one is 'moved'. According to Kant: 'This movement (especially in its inception) may be compared to a vibration, i.e., to a rapidly alternating repulsion from and attraction to one and the same object'. Human imagination, words and pictures, fail us in the face of the sublime: 'What is excessive for the imagination . . . is as it were an abyss' (Kant and Guyer, 2000, p. 141). To the category of the sublime is attributed not only the uplifting and the pure, but also the inexpressible. For philosopher Jean-François Lyotard, the sublime motivates the avant-garde painter in enabling the viewer to see 'only by making it impossible to see', or to 'please only by causing pain' (1986, p. 78), important among the functions of art, and philosophy. *Chora* is sublime in that it also resists description.

The concept of the sublime in turn brings to mind the idea of the threshold. The Latin for 'threshold' is *limen*, a word stem that appears in variation in several words. The *subliminal* pertains to thought that is below the threshold of consciousness (Freud, 1991, p. 163). To *sublimate* is to push into unconsciousness. It is a term still used in chemistry, in which a solid substance turns into a vapour without melting, or a vapour condenses into a solid without passing through the liquid phase. The sublime is a condition that undercuts, or exceeds, the threshold (between solid, liquid and gas). In this the sublime is a transgression, a boundary crossing, the indeterminate condition reached at the limit. It also connotes tarrying at the edge, lingering at the edge of an abyss.

Derrida associates *chora* with the phenomenon of *mise en abyme*, which means 'putting into infinity', or standing at an abyss or chasm, the effect you get when standing between two parallel facing mirrors and look into the infinitely receding reflections. *Mise en abyme* is evident where a picture appears within a picture, or the dreamer encounters a dream within a dream. Elsewhere Derrida also uses the term to account for the interreferentiality of texts (intertextuality).

Edges and boundaries mark moments of entry and exit. The *chora* implies a particular movement. Modern Greek preserves *hypodoche* (receptacle) as

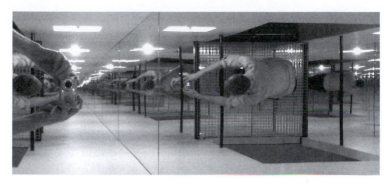

Mirror room. Aaros Aarhus Kunstmuseum, Denmark.

'reception' or 'welcome'. A visitor is received in the reception hall and usually departs by the same route. A place of reception is also one of departure. You put things into a receptacle and also take things out. The movement over the line implies a return. This simple narrative structure of excursion and return recurs throughout myth, storytelling, ritual practices and architecture. It is not just that the putative traveller is caught up in a repetitive sequence of goings and comings, but that she is transformed in the process. Excursions from Edinburgh to Paris are repeated time and again, but each time Paris is different because I (the tourist) am transformed through my experiences of my home city, and my impression and understanding of Edinburgh is transformed by my excursions to Paris. With enough travel, I, along with myriad other tourists, also effect transformation in the places we visit. In any case I see Paris through the filter of my home. According to sociologist John Urry, the experience of the tourist 'renders extraordinary, activities that otherwise would be mundane and everyday' (1990, p. 13) by virtue of being in another place. There is pleasure in eating as I usually eat but at a café on the Boulevard Saint-Germain rather than my own dining room or in front of the television; or to walk as I usually walk, but through Le Marais or along the banks of the Seine.

Something of this transformative aspect of *chora*, as a ritual encounter with different spaces, is illuminated by architectural theorist Alberto Pérez-Gómez in his article 'Chora: The space of architectural representation'. Drawing on Plato's *Timaeus*, here *chora* is 'the space of human creation and participation' and 'an invisible ground' existing beyond language and yet makes language and culture possible (Pérez-Gómez, 1994, p. 9). As a 'space for contemplation and a space of participation' (Pérez-Gómez, 1994, p. 15), *chora*'s functioning is given embodiment in theatre: the place of the chorus, choreography and other concepts shared with *chora*. Pérez-Gómez also identifies *chora* as a kind of bastard offspring of the domestic goddess Hestia and Hermes, the god of mobility and thresholds (Pérez-Gómez, 1994, p. 9). I would add that Hermes is the messenger god, responsible for interpretation, hermeneutics. He is also the confuser of distinctions, and a trickster (Hyde, 1998). By this reading *chora* embraces concepts of excursion, ritual and ambiguity.

The anthropologist Victor Turner writes about initiation rituals as pertaining to the condition of being at an intermediate stage in a rite of passage, a position of confusion, ambiguity and paradox (Turner, 1967). The initiate returns from the experience transformed. There is a crossing point, something you dip into and emerge from. Entering and leaving, excursion and return, ritual repetition, encounters with otherness, suggest leaving a mark, a trace, the perpetuation of dynamic living transformation that is being and becoming. It is also a process of hybridity, ambiguation and confusion.

But as if to frustrate our conception of this third realm even further, Derrida highlights another particular characteristic of *chora*. *Chora* seems to break from the principles of entering and leaving, of leaving a mark, of giving something back from a spatial exchange. It receives the forms and gives place to them. But in so doing it remains unchanged by them. If *chora* is female receiving the male forms then it remains virginal (Derrida, 1997, p. 17). Once the malleable clay has received the imprint of a stamp it can be rolled up and used again. The original impression is easily erased, without trace. Lest we think of *chora* as memory-enriched, multilayered, deeply symbolic and sign-filled, under Derrida's scrutiny it is nothing of the kind. The substrate of our being is indifferent to what has gone before. *Chora* 'gives nothing' (Derrida, 1997, p. 18).

Space and paradox

What are architects to make of *chora*, as interpreted by various scholars and in particular by Derrida? The two realms advanced by Plato, the distinction Plato makes between the Intelligible and the Sensible, and any philosophy or architecture built upon the distinction, are rendered problematic or, worse, invalid, as they seem to rely, according to Plato, the founder of the distinction, on a spurious and illogical entity, namely *chora*. Few theorists or historians of architecture would thereby dismiss Plato, or his influence, with or without Derrida.

Derrida draws on and contributes to a tradition of reflection, the role of radical flux and indeterminacy, that is evident in remnant form in Plato's writing. Prior to Plato, the pre-Socratics had assumed the centrality of paradox and contradiction. For Heraclitus, 'Things taken together are whole and not whole, something which is being brought together and brought apart, which is in tune and out of tune' (Allen, 1985, p. 41). We are also heirs to Aristotle's principles of logic, including the law of the excluded middle, which seems to challenge such illogicality, that something could be both the case and not the case at the same time, the cause and caused by (Allen, 1985, p. 330).

Thinking about reality as a paradoxical play appears in many traditions, as outlined by the religious philosopher Mircea Eliade in the case of rituals and legends. He notes that certain rites and beliefs have the aim of reminding human kind that 'the ultimate reality, the sacred, the divine, defy all possibilities of rational comprehension'. They remind us that such realities 'can only be grasped as a mystery or a paradox, that the divine conception cannot be conceived as a sum of qualities and virtues but as an absolute freedom, beyond Good and Evil' (Eliade, 1965, p. 82). The Jewish philosopher Gershom Scholem offers a similar characterisation of the writings of the Kabbalah in the medieval Jewish tradition. The Kabbalah highlighted aspects of God that were 'beyond rationality' and which become paradoxical the moment they are put into words (Scholem, 1955, p. 225). As outlined by Eliade, the symbolic reversal of roles, the suspension of laws and customs under the pretext of carnival pranks, and orgiastic rituals seek 'a reintegration of opposites, a regression to the primordial and homogeneous', but such activities are also 'a symbolic restoration of "Chaos," of the undifferentiated unity that preceded the Creation' (Scholem, 1955, p. 114).

Such paradox also finds expression in the tradition of verbal nonsense, to which surrealism was a party in the twentieth century. According to theorist of fantasy literature Martin Esslin, verbal paradox is 'a striving to enlarge and to transcend the limits of the material universe and its logic'. Nonsense attempts 'the destruction of language – through nonsense' (1961, pp. 245, 248), as developed by Lewis Carroll and later by James Joyce.

Jacques Lacan, theorist and psychoanalyst to a number of Surrealist artists, lectured and wrote about reality as riven by paradox and 'contradictory determinations' (Žižek, 1989, p. 171). At the pen of Gilles Deleuze, such reflections speak of the residency of the real in the workings of schizophrenia (Deleuze and Guattari, 1977, p. 311). The task of the psychotic subversive is to act through proliferation, juxtaposition and disjunction, in opposition to building structures, and subdividing into pyramidal hierarchisation.

I have already mentioned concepts of the sublime, a means of accounting for spatial experience that defies expression or representation. There is also the experience of the uncanny, a concept developed by Freud in which repeated encounters remind us of what it was to be a child and believe in magic, developed also through the concept of haunting (Freud, 1990; Vidler, 1995). To this typology of other spaces we can add heterotopias, as coined by Foucault, which are simultaneously here and not here (Foucault, 1986), as when on a mobile phone in a railway carriage. As outlined by anthropologist Marc Augé, there are also non-places (Augé, 1995), those places where we have to prove our innocence, such as the sign-laden, unhomely and transitional places of airport security zones, freeway ramps and checkpoints. The radical point of these spatial characterisations is not only that we need to attend to the aberrant in spatial experience, but that space has its origins in such properties, in the character of *chora*. *Chora* is all of these spatial constructs (the sublime, the uncanny, non-place, heterotopias, other places) by a different name. Derrida has provided a service to the authors of these otherwise marginal and ambiguous constructions of space by demonstrating the presence of such spaces at the heart of reasoned and rational spatiality.

The radical point of these spatial characterisations is not only that we need to attend to the aberrant in spatial experience, but that space has its origins in such properties, in the character of *chora*.

Derrida's interpretation of *chora* joins with various other strategies in opening up a space, generating new metaphors, for architecture, and dispensing with old ones. I return to my pragmatic attitude to this tradition, and that of Derrida, via Richard Rorty: 'It takes a lot of hard work' to manage dialectical inversions, turning things on their head, identifying and elevating contradiction and paradox (1989, p. 134). The implication here is that Derrida's intellectual process is more important than the conclusions he reaches. The labour required to get there is the reward, not the goal. The effort required to identify and justify *chora* is more rewarding than representing it. *Chora* is emblematic of a radical orientation to knowledge, and therefore to architecture. Derrida's place as a radical thinker is the subject of the next chapter.

CHAPTER 6

Derrida and Radical Practice

In his essay 'Archive fever', Derrida links institutions with the need to keep records: '*every* archive . . . is at once *institutive* and *conservative*' (Derrida and Prenowitz, 1995, p. 12). Institutions, such as government departments, hospitals, churches, schools, professional institutes, architectural organisations and, of course, universities, are at the apogee of the impulse to conserve. Institutions exist to get things done, but also to preserve and conserve, an obvious necessity when we note that institutions typically outlive their office-holders, governors and employees. The maintenance of records becomes a major instrument by which institutions perpetuate themselves, and is crucial in any institution's functioning. Architecture is complicit in this institutional role. In so far as architects produce buildings, their activities sustain and conserve the functions of banks, schools, hospitals, corporations and other institutional structures. Architecture also has institutional presence.

The impulse to conserve equates to a kind of *conservatism*, a term which has many meanings in everyday usage. In politics, conservatism promotes the importance and preservation of traditional institutions, including a return to how things used to be, traditional values, or simply affords resistance to change. A conservative view of architecture might similarly elevate in importance the role of keeping the archive, the architectural canon, prime examples of what constitutes good architecture, but also to conserve, revive and promote what architecture sees as its core values, authority structures and rules. There are many demonstrations of the conservative impulse in architecture. The rationalist, as conservative, might equate to the classicist, asserting that architecture conforms to natural laws and is subject to the authority of geometrical and enduring principles of reason (Colquhoun, 1989). Traditionally this meant preserving the classical rules of proportion. In more modern guise the rationalist may advance the view that architecture is determined by functional requirements (form follows function), or an adherence to objectivity, scientific detachment and rational method.

Historically, the Romantics thought of themselves as free spirits, as if to counter the dominance of a stodgy adherence to Classicism. Rousseau, as Romantic, sought to be 'free and virtuous, superior to fortune and opinion, and independent of all exterior circumstances' (Rousseau, 2008, Book VIII). But free spirits can purvey conservative traits. The Romantic, as conservative, under the guise of free-spirited adventurism, may cling to the authority of charismatic and eccentric leaders, particular architectural canons, or notions of an originary source to architectural creation, and the concept of genius and celebrity, commonly invested in key design leaders, constituting a kind of conservative subjectivity. Ayn Rand's approving presentation of the fictional architect Howard Roark in the novel *The Fountainhead* (1972) has come to epitomise such a conceit, that of the maverick free thinker struggling against mediocrity. On the one hand Roark stands for the rights of the common man, while on the other hand he eschews the greyness of ordinary tastes imposed by bureaucrats who have their eye on the bottom line. Rand's hero after all wishes to conserve individual achievement above society as a whole.

Of course, conservatism runs through every aspect of social life. Most people will want to preserve things they hold as important, but as any voter knows there are those who more readily deploy the cause of conservation as a rallying cry. Even Derrida could be cast as a 'conservative' in that he was a staunch supporter of the policy of retaining the teaching of philosophy in French schools, held to academic rigour and seemed to enjoy his status as a contributor to the contemporary intellectual canon as a celebrity philosopher. By several accounts, and in keeping with the careers of many intellectuals, Derrida enjoyed his position in the limelight and the authority his work commanded in certain quarters, but his is not a philosophy of charismatic leadership. It would be hard to reconcile Derrida's thinking with any kind of intellectual conservatism, especially as we consider his determined challenge to orthodox distinctions and priorities, concepts of foundations, fundamentals, origins and other metaphysical precepts.

It would be hard to reconcile Derrida's thinking with any kind of intellectual conservatism

Conservatism is also traditionally contrasted with liberalism: ostensibly a willingness for and commitment to change, experimentation, challenge and a distancing from reliance on hierarchies and the canons of what is regarded by some elite group as right and proper conduct. Traditionally, liberalism pursues a social arrangement where people are free to advance their own good so long as individuals 'do not attempt to deprive others of theirs' (Mill, 1991, p. 14). There are clearly those who advocate and rally behind the cause of liberalism. In architecture, such an advanced liberal orientation may involve opening up the design process to the users of buildings (Hill, 2003) as well as to clients, consulting with a wide range of stakeholders, self-criticism by those facilitating changes in the built environment, or focusing on providing for under-represented groups rather than seeking to preserve the interests of existing institutions or those with the most power.

The thinking of Karl Marx (1818–1883) and the political reformers of the nineteenth and twentieth centuries are representative of a particular brand of liberalism. Marxism pits itself against conservative elements in society, characterising conservatives as those with an investment in land, buildings, machines and the financial reserves to sustain them, i.e. the capital of industry that belongs to the dominating bourgeois class. Traditional Marxism aims for the overturning of capitalism by the grassroots action of labour, the culmination of a struggle between the classes: 'brutal contradiction, the shock of body against body' (Marx, 1977, p. 215). Marx's thinking is developed within the intellectual movement known as Critical Theory (Feenberg, 2002), which presents a perpetual scepticism towards claims of social improvement. The Critical Theorists seek constantly to uncover the all-pervasive and pernicious hand of capitalism that inevitably favours the ruling elite and perpetuates (conserves) the class system. In fact, Critical Theorists attack liberalism itself as pluralistic and uncommitted. Key Critical Theorists also belonged to the Frankfurt School, a group of European intellectuals who fled Germany for New

York in the 1930s, a movement whose influence is well-represented by Theodor Adorno (Adorno, 1991), Walter Benjamin (Benjamin, 1992) and Herbert Marcuse (Marcuse, 1991). The group drew from Marx, Freudian psychoanalytic theory and Structuralism, and their legacy is still evident in architectural theory and studio practice.

Manfredo Tafuri has been a foremost proponent of a critical position in architecture (Tafuri, 1996). The thinking of the Critical Theorists, many of whom were members of the Communist Party, was a dominant intellectual force in Paris in the 1960s and 1970s. Though inevitably in their intellectual company, Derrida eventually distanced himself from this group, which accounts in part for his lukewarm assimilation into French intellectual life in the early part of his career (Mikics, 2010, pp. 156, 213) and the charge made by some that Derrida's work provides little impetus for social or political reform, a charge that he sought to redress in the 1990s. It is accurate to position Derrida within liberal intellectual life, though he was not among the Critical Theorists (Mikics, 2010, p. 213).

It is accurate to position Derrida within liberal intellectual life, though he was not among the Critical Theorists

As we have seen, the legacy on which Derrida drew was in fact Phenomenology, through Husserl and Heidegger, of whom he could be said to have been a fully engaged and even sympathetic critic, though he departed from one of their leading protégés, Hans-Georg Gadamer (1900–2002) (Gadamer, 1975). There is insufficient space to summarise what Phenomenology stands for here, but for our purposes, at least as represented by Gadamer, it presents as a 'moderate' position within the liberal spectrum (Gallagher, 1992). It is an altogether more optimistic position than that held by the Critical Theorists, trusting of individuals and communities and less motivated by the political imperative to provoke reform or revolution. It seeks rather to understand, and to understand how we understand. This moderate attitude focuses on the art of doing and making, not just making objects and texts, but in building communities of practice, support for which emerges from debates within philosophy, particularly on the theme of how it is we come to know what is true, i.e. theories of knowledge, epistemology or, more specifically, interpretation. I alluded to these communities of practice and the diffusion of influence in Chapter 1. This moderate, Phenomenological position finds ready connection with Pragmatism, which I also referenced in the Prologue to this book.

So this crude map of the intellectual landscape suggests a terrain of thought with several regions. The conservative corner is driven by the need to discover, conserve and preserve standards, knowledge and values. This region can be occupied both by rationalists who submit their models of reason to the rigours of rule, order, objectivity and scientific method, and the Romantics, who emphasise individuality, genius and the power of imagination. The landscape is made more complex by a path that leads from the Romantics, among whom Rousseau was a leading figure, to the social reformers and liberals of the nineteenth century. After all, Rousseau's philosophy was enlisted in support of the French Revolution. Among such liberal influences we have the socialists, political reformers, Marx, and later the twentieth-century Critical Theorists. The moderates were less motivated by reform, a view that becomes clearer as we consider the nature of interpretation in the following section.

So my aim in this chapter is to position Derrida's thinking in relation to these various twentieth-century philosophical positions, particularly in casting Derrida as a 'radical', a term ascribed to his thinking by the philosopher John Caputo (Caputo, 1987). Clearly Derrida's thinking is radical, when compared to various conservative positions, which in turn reflects on Derrida's view of the role of institutions, and the implications for the institution of architecture.

Interpretation

As it looms large in the landscape of language, and the understanding of texts, we will focus here on interpretation. This discourse takes its cue from Phenomenology, which after all has little regard for the Structuralist problematic of the play between signifier and signified. In pragmatic mode, the

Phenomenologist Martin Heidegger sees signs simply as equipment (1962, p. 108), and later on he constructs his discourse about language as 'the house of Being' (1971). Interpretation gets to the heart of who we are as human beings in the world: how do we interpret the world? Interpretation is of obvious importance in architecture. Architects interpret the client brief, sets of requirements, regulations, drawings and the site, and generate responses that could be regarded as interpretations. These items are themselves interpretations of certain conditions. A building design is arguably an interpretation of a set of requirements, needs and social and physical conditions. Buildings are also there to be interpreted and critiqued. I develop the theme of interpretation in architecture in a book co-authored with Adrian Snodgrass: *Interpretation in Architecture* (Snodgrass and Coyne, 2006). There we showed the ubiquity of interpretation, and design as interpretation.

Prior to his engagement with architecture, Derrida tackled the issue of interpretation, or at least he entered into a debate with Hans-Georg Gadamer, one of the foremost proponents of interpretation as a ubiquitous human activity (Gadamer, 1975). The word commonly used for the study of interpretation is 'hermeneutics'. Through his alignment with Phenomenology and with Heidegger, Gadamer has been identified by some as a proponent of a 'moderate hermeneutics' (Gallagher, 1992). Gadamer's theory is basically that in any interpretative situation, such as reading and trying to understand a book, comprehending a work of art or appreciating a piece of music, we arrive redolent with expectations. Without these anticipations and projections, derived from our personal history, engagement with the values and norms of a community and prior experience, we would not be able to interpret anything. As an interpreter of architecture, on my first encounter with a new building, I expect a certain experience. Inevitably my expectations are rarely met and so I have to adjust my expectations in light of the encounter. This adjustment constitutes a to-and-fro movement, a game, a play within any interpretative situation. At least, this is interpretation that is open, free and engaged. In any interpretive encounter I, the viewer or participant, am transformed. My horizon of expectations changes, so that I will probably come to my next interpretative encounter with a new set of expectations. Interpretation is also a process of personal transformation, of learning, of education, of edification. I alluded to this process in the context of the threshold in the previous chapter. The role of interpreter and tourist (or pilgrim) coalesce: interpretation involves excursion into the text and a return transformed.

In fact, the characterisation I have given so far of the intellectual constellation or landscape in which we are seeking to position Derrida is derived largely from philosopher Shaun Gallagher's astute description of the field of interpretation theory (Gallagher, 1992). For Gallagher there are four intellectual zones: conservative, critical, moderate and radical, which I followed in the previous section. These correspond loosely to four positions on interpretation. Gadamer's *moderate* hermeneutics contrasts with a more conservative view, which is that the purpose of literature, art, architecture is to conserve and transmit meanings (Betti, 1990). So, according to conservatives interpretation really involves uncovering and discovering truths that are somehow fixed. In the case of art, that might typically involve a quest for the intentions of the artists or author in creating the work in the first place. The final arbiter in the matter of the interpretation of a work of art is what the artist meant by the work, which in the case of a historical work involves comparing and sifting evidence to uncover these authorial intentions, and of course debating the evidence of such intentions. Such a view might also promote the principle of reason adumbrated by Rene Descartes, that it is necessary to approach any philosophical problem (or interpretative situation) with a clear mind, i.e. without prejudice (Descartes, 1968). This conservative approach suggests the possibility of an immediacy of contact between the text, art work, building and the viewer, or access to an essence pertaining to the object that is independent of the viewing situation, and to a fundamental that is there to be uncovered.

Gadamer stands against such a conservative hermeneutics. Such essences and intentions are notoriously elusive. In any case, a work of art means what it means to us today, and in the context of its reception. There is no final authority on what the work means, short of that claimed by interpreters operating within an interpretive community. The interpretive process and its derivation through communities of conversationalists never ends. Individuals and communities are

Graffiti exhibition, Fondation Cartier pour l'Art Contemporain. Architect: Jean Nouvel, Paris.

constantly reinterpreting and challenging their own and each other's interpretations, developing new interpretative practices, new modes of legitimating what they believe. Communities also interact, as if to fuse their horizons, as when the values of elite art establishments meet street culture to generate a new street-wise elite: graffiti artists, YouTube creatives, flash mob animateurs. Communities take many forms: two people in conversation, cliques of friends, social networks, factions, art movements, political groups, special interest groups, trades and professions, as well as formalised professional communities, such as the Royal Institute of British Architects (RIBA), the Royal Incorporation of Architects in Scotland (RIAS), the Royal Australian Institute of Architects (RAIA), and of course architecture schools.

Radical hermeneutics

Though much that is radical may emerge from the hermeneutical encounters between radically disparate groups, Derrida departs from this moderate position to form a fourth intellectual stance, that philosopher John Caputo regards as a 'radical hermeneutics'. Derrida and Gadamer articulated their differences in a series of debates (Michelfelder and Palmer, 1989). The idea of interpretive communities is too cosy for Derrida, relying too much on the good will among participants for interpretation to work, and such bonhomie cannot always be assumed. Furthermore, interpreters are not only driven by expectations. The moderate hermeneutical metaphor is always of facing forward, of expectation, projecting ahead of oneself. Derrida asserts that circumstances do not necessarily confront us in this way, but surprise us, from behind as it were. This is Derrida's opening proposition in a documentary film about his life: 'For me that is the real future, that which is unpredictable, the Other who comes without me being able to await it' (Dick and Ziering Kofman, 2002). As implied in the debate, and as inferred by Caputo, Derrida's radical hermeneutics draws attention to the element of surprise, ruptures in the fabric of our horizons, breaches in the workings of community.

There are similarities here with a 'critical hermeneutics'. The neo-Marxist position focuses on the target of interpretation. Any interpretive task worth the effort requires uncovering class exploitation, hegemony, in an interpretive situation. So in examining, critiquing, i.e. interpreting, a social housing project, the neo-Marxist may look for the dominance of capitalism, the means by which people are excluded as well as included, the urban politics in play and so on. This is a hermeneutics of suspicion, according to Paul Ricoeur (1970).

But the radical position seeks to turn ideas on their head, to unsettle certainties and established modes of practice. As outlined in Chapter 1, I think of the Surrealists and their progeny in this light, as they would wrest objects, ideas and propositions from their usual context and project them into a new context. Architecture has produced many studio experiments as the impetus for radical design, such as the members of the firm Coop Himmelblau's use of their own digital portraits as the impetus for the design for a new town and Tschumi's deployment of 'useless' but expensive follies in the Parc de la Villette as the core of an architectural proposition. We can think of these experiments as radical in the processes deployed, in their outcomes and rhetorics, and in some cases in the modes of practice they deploy.

Within this intellectual landscape, radical intellectualism is not the exclusive preserve of Derrida. To it we can add Jacques Lacan (1901–1981), as well as Gilles Deleuze (1925–1995), Michel Serres (1930–) and others who have influenced architecture.

Institutions

As indicated at the beginning of this chapter, Derrida addresses the issue of conservatism, or at least the impulse to conserve, in his essay 'Archive fever' (Derrida and Prenowitz, 1995). The essay was adapted from a lecture, delivered at the Freud archives in London. Freud of course made much of the phenomenon of remembering, recollection, the recovery of lost memories, so the issue of the archive triggers for Derrida a host of intertextual associations and connections implicating Freud. Not least among them is an apparent contradiction in the notion of the archive. For Derrida, the archive is both 'revolutionary and traditional' (Derrida and Prenowitz, 1995, p. 12).

> **Consequence: right on what permits and conditions archivization, we will never find anything other than what exposes to destruction, in truth what menaces with destruction introducing, *a priori*, forgetfulness and the archiviolithic into the heart of the monument. Into the 'by heart' itself. The archive always works, and *a priori*, against itself.**
>
> **(Derrida and Prenowitz, 1995, p. 14)**

One key to identifying contradiction in the archive is to note that we store things away to absolve us from the necessity to remember them. I write things down not so that I can remember but to give me licence to forget. The internal activity that is memory gets transferred to some memory substitute, an external medium. As explained by one reviewer of Derrida's essay, the impulse to create an archive is 'both a fever to save – to impress into a substrate – and a fever to destroy – to print out onto a substrate' (Lawlor, 1998, pp. 796–798). Drawing on Freud's concepts of the pleasure principle and the death drive, Derrida asserts that an archive involves a desire to safeguard information for the internal consumption and edification of the individual, contrasted with the need to expose information to the outside for the benefit of others. In order to conserve you have in effect to destroy the thing you want to conserve by exposing it to the outside world.

But what resonates most with architectural concerns is again Derrida's clever reversion to the productive strategy of intertextuality, the linking together of ostensibly unlikely terms and references. He has already brought the idea of the institution into the realms of text. What are archives after all but piles and boxes of documents? But there are further links with architecture. Derrida indicates that the word 'archive' was originally deployed in Greek and Latin to denote the residence or home of the senior office bearer. As we saw in Chapter 3, the prefix 'archi' in fact pertains to the first in authority, as in the case of 'architect', the master builder, a term that also relates to 'arche' (*arkhe*): rule, order and law. This is one of the ways that Derrida deals with conservatism, as a problematic and contradictory issue that pertains to texts, institutions and buildings.

the word 'archive' was originally deployed in Greek and Latin to denote the residence or home of the senior office bearer

Let us return to the conservative, moderate, critical and radical constellation of intellectual thought outlined above. The radical ground for dealing with institutions has arguably been dominated by doctrines against rule (*an-arche*), licensing further suggestive linguistic relations with architecture as 'anarchitecture' (Evans, 1970). The anarchists quite simply proposed the extinction of institutions. The famous anarchist Peter Kropotkin (1842–1921) proclaimed in the nineteenth century that freedom is to emerge from 'the ruins and rubbish of old institutions and old superstitions' (Kropotkin and Shatz, 1995). Equality and fairness for all 'cannot be brought about by Acts of Parliament, but only by taking immediate and effective possession of all that is necessary to ensure the well-being of all' (Kropotkin and Shatz, 1995, p. 23). The answer lay in communism, but a 'Communism without government – the Communism of the Free'. Hope lay in the establishment of 'mutual agreement' and a commonality of purpose as a means to self-regulation in place of law.

Derrida had no such contempt for institutions. One of his institutional causes was the Collège international de philosophie (Ciph), which he co-founded in 1983, as an institute to promote the preservation of the teaching of philosophy in secondary schools. Derrida elaborates on the nature of this and other institutions in an address to Cornell University in the early 1980s. Here Derrida advocates the primacy of thought over knowledge, proposing that universities preserve their role as 'communities of thought'. For Derrida, and in keeping with the elevation of *thought* by Hegel and Heidegger, thought is 'a dimension that is not reducible to technique, nor to science, nor to philosophy' (1983, p. 16).

> Now reason is only one species of thought – which does not mean that thought is 'irrational'. Such a community would interrogate the essence of reason and of the principle of reason, the values of the basic, of the principial, of radicality, of the *arkhe* in general, and it would attempt to draw out all the possible consequences of this questioning. It is not certain that such thinking can bring together a community or found an institution in the traditional sense of these words. What is meant by community and institution must be rethought. This thinking must also unmask – an infinite task – all the ruses of end-orienting reason, the paths by which apparently disinterested research can find itself indirectly reappropriated, reinvested by programs of all sorts.
>
> (Derrida, 1983, p. 16)

Derrida here advocates a 'double gesture': on the one hand upholding 'professional rigour and competence' and on the other hand 'going as far as possible, theoretically and practically, in the most directly underground thinking about the abyss beneath the university'. The university has to deal with 'the barrier against the abyss, the abyss against the barrier' (Derrida, 1983, p. 17). Radicalism is risky, not in that it might lead to social unrest, the destruction of institutions, but that it becomes the norm. The risk here is that such radicality ends up being appropriated, i.e. it becomes institutionalised as the right way to think. The task for the institution is to grasp this risk:

metaphysics, what I have here called 'thought' risks in its turn (but I believe this risk is unavoidable – it is the risk of the future itself) being reappropriated by socio-political forces that could find it in their own interest in certain situations.

(Derrida, 1983, p. 17)

John Caputo elaborates on Derrida's theme, affirming that Derrida's approach to the role of institutions is subversive but not irrational (Caputo, 1987, p. 234). He translates Derrida's insights to the 'double gesture': combining professional rigour and competence with the subversion of the foundations of the professions: 'Institutions are the way things get done, and they are prone to violence.... Nothing is innocent' (Caputo, 1987, p. 234). For Caputo, Derrida liberates reason by emancipating it from the necessity to appeal to foundations, principle and other 'metaphysical prejudices'. Derrida wants to redescribe reason, not to 'jettison' it (Caputo, 1987, pp. 209–210).

Derrida is in the company of other radical thinkers in his advocacy of attending to the indeterminate in institutional life. As Karl Marx was not against capitalism, but saw within it the seeds of its own destruction (Marx, 1977), so thinkers such as Deleuze and Guattari see that institutions contain their own forces for subversion, from within. Institutions, the necessary structures of civil society, are tree-like, hierarchical, with a main stem that supports the rest. But they are also prone to infestation from rhizomic, fungal intrusions that are parasitic on established structures. The rhizome grows from within to subvert the edifice (Deleuze and Guattari, 1988, p. 15). Derrida concurs that institutions are prone to disturbances to their own operations and authority from within, an attribute that needs to be sustained.

Activism and the radicalisation of architectural practices

How do we align Derrida's radicality with what we might think of the radical in architecture? According to Miles Glendinning's critical history of modernism, Deconstructive architecture borrowed from 1920s Expressionism, but with 'an anarchy of jagged, exploding "shards", with straight lines broken up and flat surfaces twisted and tangled' (2010, p. 61). Derrida clearly has more to contribute to radical understandings of the institution of architecture than to the creation of radical shapes and forms, or the transposition of conventional architectural elements. There seems little that is institutionally radical about the way architecture absorbed Derrida in the 1980s and 1990s, or about Derrida's encounter with Eisenman.

There seems little that is institutionally radical about the way architecture absorbed Derrida in the 1980s and 1990s, or about Derrida's encounter with Eisenman.

As a variant of anarchism, it is activism that seems to have claimed the ground of a radical approach to institutions, though largely from outside them. Activism takes many forms, but gains prominence as a strategic approach to social reform that operates outside state political structures. It goes beyond protest, resistance and revolution. According to *The Activist's Handbook*, 'today's activists use strategy and tactics to triumph in their campaign for change' (Shaw, 2001, p. 2). Activists might appropriate the very instruments they seek to reform. Such tactics are brought into sharp relief in relation to advertising and the mass media, sometimes described as 'culture jamming', the use of commercial advertising strategies against capitalism itself. For commentator and journalist Naomi Klein: 'The most sophisticated culture jams are not stand-alone parodies but interceptions – counter-messages that hack into a corporation's own method of communication to send a message starkly at odds with the one that was intended.' This is a process that forces the target company to pay to have the intrusion ejected, in other words the company has to 'foot the bill for its own subversion' (Klein, 2005, p. 281). Of course, ad campaigners also play on the culture of subversion: 'there are no rebels who cannot be tamed with an ad campaign or by a street promoter who really speaks to them' (Klein, 2005, p. 300). Activism at its most sophisticated is a knowing enterprise, aware of its place in a spiral of moves and countermoves, deploying the resources of the mass media and news reporting, as well as 'viral' techniques, events and flash

Activism and anarchy. G8 street protest, Edinburgh 2007.

mobs, for purveying action and opinion through online social networks and whatever media are to hand.

Architecture has long participated in such moves. Think of the user-participation social housing projects of the architect Ralph Erskine (1914–2005) and others. The book *Urban Act* revives and radicalises the theme by articulating how urban activism 'can take different forms: from radical opposition and criticism to a more constructive and propositional acting, embedded in everyday life' (PEVRAV, 2008, p. 11). The participative and community-oriented design projects outlined in the book seek to challenge 'both academic, professional, artistic, and political practice' by addressing 'the creativity and criticality of a new approach to the city'. This approach is necessarily heterogeneous and 'reflects a multiplicity of viewpoints and ways of doing'. So such radical practices

Parodic advertising. Advertising poster, Munich, Germany.

involve bringing together artists, media activists, neighbourhood organisations and software designers. Such confederations seem to seek a diffusion of professional expertise by showing architects, urbanists and educators as participants in heteroglot teams rather than privileged experts with authoritative roles.

The concerns and strategies of urban activism are also local rather than universal, dealing with specifics rather than globally applicable solutions to problems. The strength of such groupings is that they 'are highly specific and have the quality of reinventing uses and practices in ways that traditional professional structures cannot afford (due to their generic functioning)'. Expertise that is not ready to hand in the local context is characterised as 'extra-local' rather than global or international. Such an approach contrasts with that of the well-meaning but over-scaled systems approaches of the founders of the 1970s think tank, the Club of Rome, tackling population growth as 'the Predicament of Mankind' (Meadows *et al.*, 1972). The emphasis in contemporary activism is of course on the urban, and urban interventions, rather than buildings and architecture. The design and construction of a building may or may not constitute an appropriate outcome of an activist intervention. The claim is that such urban practices are ' "tactical", "situational" and "active", based on soft professional and artistic skills and civic informal structures, which can adapt themselves to changing urban situations that are critical, reactive and creative enough to produce real change' (PEVRAV, 2008, p. 11).

Such projects might include the establishment of farms in inner urban areas, the creation of community centres and events, public artworks, systems for recycling materials to create new urban facilities, but it is the processes that are of most interest, the way marginal groups might be empowered to have a say in the way their environments are formed, bringing together diverse stakeholders and interacting with authority structures. The mood is one of protest, building on the demonstrations of the 1960s against 'the repressive and coercive order of the transnational corporations and institutions' in the words of theorist and activist Brian Holmes (2008, p. 302). The new motif is that of the subversive carnival aided by Internet communications. So the carnival is able to orchestrate on a global scale, a 'do-it-yourself geopolitics', as in the case of radical protests scheduled to coincide with meetings of world leaders (the G8 summits).

The intellectual authority for such tactics draws substantially on the urban practices of the Situationists (de Zegher and Wigley, 2001) and the sociologist Michel de Certeau in *The Practice of Everyday Life* (1984), as well as the writings of Foucault, Henri Lefebvre, Deleuze and Guaratti. As well as their advocacy of rhizomic interventions, Deleuze and Guattari champion the singular and specific against the universal, and present such tactics through disruptive metaphors of nomads, frictions between tectonic plates, runaway machines, bodies without organs, parasitism and schizophrenia (Deleuze and Guattari, 1988; Ballantyne, 2007). Derrida is only evident at the periphery of such citation lists, but his approaches to institutions and language have direct relevance to urban activism, and as I raised in a previous chapter, one can only wonder what would have happened to the Parc de la Villette insertion project, and to the reputation of Deconstruction in architecture, had Derrida been teamed with architects with activist leanings.

In so far as urban activism seeks to reverse certain privileged oppositions and hierarchies, it engages in a game that is linguistic, and therefore subject to explanation and critique through Derridean analysis. Displacing the sole expert by the group, top-down command by grass-roots empowerment, universals by specifics. Such linguistic tactics, which also correlate with certain actions, fall prey to the privileging of which Derrida speaks in his characterisations of speech versus writing. Grass-roots activism already alludes to an authentic core, a tribal and somewhat natural order of immediacy and engagement. Problems arise in activism in the insistence on 'real change' (PEVRAV, 2008, p. 11), as if people can know or agree on what it is they are seeking to change and what they want to change it to. In so far as activism perpetuates its own restlessness, then it garners approval from Derridean analysis. As soon as it becomes complacent about its own motives, or the obviousness of its causes, then it relinquishes its claim to radicality, at least in Derrida's terms.

Derrida's claim to radicalism therefore involves acquiescence to the inevitability of the *aporia*, the problematic, the restlessness of indeterminacy. Such an acceptance does not imply that one does not do anything, a kind of do-nothing nihilism, but implies the necessity of continued dialogue and action. In so far as such action might appeal to an ideal, such as justice for all, empowerment of the marginalised, the fair distribution of resources, core values, agreement among stakeholders, then that is a shifting core.

Radical pedagogy

Education provides a fruitful route to the exploration of urban activism and in turn to Derridean radicalism. In many respects universities provide a model for practice, and for architectural practice. As universities provide the entry point for most professionals, it is tempting to think of universities as responsible for the dissemination and perpetuation of professional practice. Of course, universities also respond to practice, and are sometimes in conflict with business practices and aspirations.

The 1980s saw the introduction of Derrida's Deconstruction to the study of literature. There was as much interest in his approach to literature, and his ways of writing, as in his philosophical conclusions about metaphysics. Literary studies are primarily concerns of the academy. So Deconstruction is relevant to modes of education (Atkins and Johnson, 1985; Johnson, 1985; Ulmer, 1985; Zavarzadeh and Morton, 1986–1987). Educational philosopher Gregory Ulmer describes radical pedagogy in terms that resonate with political activism. Deconstructive radical pedagogy is 'to the sciences what the carnival once was to the Church' (1985, p. 61): 'In terms of curriculum, carnival disrespect means the inversion of the "order" of disciplines.' According to Ulmer, initiates into a discipline normally have to wait many years before they are exposed to the discipline's uncertainties and doubts about its own authority, the threats it is under, the unspoken challenges to its authority: 'the inner "mystery" of any discipline is not its order or coherence but is its disorder, incoherence, and arbitrariness' (1985, pp. 61–62). According to Ulmer, radical pedagogy enables the student to bypass initiation as a specialist and to confront both the grounding of a discipline, its supposed absolutes, and the provisional, destructible nature of that grounding.

As I have suggested throughout this book, the design studio of the architecture school can fulfil this role of experimentation and radical challenge, which then spills over into professional practice. For all their faults, conservatism, limitations and variation, universities and colleges as institutions provide the potential sites for the radical thought advocated by Derrida, which arguably drew him into architecture in the first place, through the academic pedagogy, writing and architectural practices of Bernard Tschumi and Peter Eisenman. The architects with whom Derrida had dealings were educators as well as practitioners. The design studio has always been a site of play, as evident in the early Bauhaus teaching approaches. The design studio also serves to demonstrate, among other things, how far removed radical Deconstructive pedagogy can be from anarchy.

So the real dangers of Deconstruction have been institutionalised within Deconstruction's own discourse. The problem for Derrida is the threat of *normalisation*. What would the deconstructive, anarchic or activist design studio be if it became the norm? According to Gallagher, 'any attempt to teach abnormal, agonistic discourse would be to normalize it and to turn it into an established discipline' (1992, p. 313). For Derrida, the worst fear is the exploitation of Deconstruction by conservatism. The perplexities that Deconstruction sets up are that the whole radical project may itself be exploited by 'socio-political forces', or 'reproducing the hierarchy' (Derrida, 1983, pp. 17, 18). As we have seen, Derrida thinks this risk is unavoidable: 'it is the risk of the future itself' (1983, p. 17).

Radical media

One of the techniques of contemporary activism is the appropriation of new media, particularly mobile phone networks and the Internet, to communicate and mobilise grass-roots action. The earliest social uses of the Internet included the formation of the WELL, the Whole Earth 'Lectronic Link, an online self-help bulletin board system created in 1985 (Rheingold, 1993). More recently mobile phone networks have played a major role in significant mass protests (Rafael, 2006). Electronic media after all support a new, variable access, user-created, highly distributed archive.

Parallel to these developments in communicability is the creation of hypertext, the interlinking of documents, evident in the interconnection between web pages. Hypertext has been taken up by some as representative of a radical decentring of texts, authoring and documentation. George Landow is one of the advocates of this way of conceiving of literature: 'We can define *hypertext* as the use of the computer to transcend the linear, bounded and fixed qualities of the traditional written text' which was, after all, 'linear, bounded and fixed' (Landow, 1994; Landow and Delany, 1994, p. 3). So a hypertextual document is cross-linked, interlinked, within itself and with other documents, so that readers can explore avenues of thought raised by the text, and even contribute comments and notes, which are in turn shared and hyperlinked.

This is what the World Wide Web has become in the twenty-first century, particularly as instantiated in Web 2.0 services such as Wikipedia, though it is characterised less by links than by search. Wikipedia is of necessity highly structured and instrumentalised, with tags, temporal markers, trace records and other devices to facilitate navigation, search and to improve confidence in the authority of the encyclopaedia entries, a true archive. So-called civic journalism, with the explosion of user-generated blogs and comments is similarly dependent on searchable databases, with entries that appear as formatted pages depending on the templates invoked. Contrary to the ideals of hypertext, readers do not seem to want free-formed, democratically disorganised text. Hypertextual linkages have been largely supplanted, at least in practice, by the ubiquitous operations of extremely rapid storage, access and formatting, with indexing and search on a massively global scale facilitated particularly through search engines such as Google. Hypertext has become a massively indexed archive of whatever gets written on the Internet. It seems to have more in common with the notion of the archive than with intertextuality.

But certain literary theorists have been keen to associate hypertext with Derrida's understanding of text and writing. As explored in previous chapters, Barbara Johnson describes Derrida's approach to the texts he is dealing with through the trope of 'intertextuality'. As we saw in Chapter 3, in his account of Plato's *Phaedrus*, and through the idea of the *pharmakon* (potion), Derrida constructs his arguments via a chain of associations, many of which go beyond what any reader would think of as the authorised meanings in the text: drug, poison, cosmetics, magician, scapegoat. Throughout his writing, Derrida makes copious and seemingly inexhaustible references that are not merely illustrative. These fine-grained, surgical investigations are not predicated on the quest for a deeper reading of a text, as if in pursuit of a core or essence, or as a probe into the unconscious of the author (Johnson, 1981). The analysis operates at the surface, or at least problematises the concept of a deep reading. As we have seen, intertextuality is a useful trope to account for Derrida's style, and it is one that resonates with certain experimental writing practice, including in architectural writing (Martin, 1990).

Derrida's concepts of intertextuality were not lost on the early advocates of hypertext. For Landow, 'hypertext creates an almost embarrassingly literal embodiment of such concepts' (Landow and Delany, 1994, p. 6). Of course, in so far as the advocacy of hypertextuality appeals to some kind of primal, authentic communicative practice, then it is subject to Derridean critique. For example, literary theorist Jay Bolter maintains that if Aristotle's or Plato's original texts were translated into hypertextual form then it becomes possible to restore to these texts something of 'their original, conversational tone' (1994, p. 116). The claim here is that hypertext gets us back to conversation and speech, which are after all more authentically human than the linear, distant and constraining process of committing thoughts to writing and print. A Derridean critique of hypertextuality shows this movement's commitment to the chimera of authentic communication, and hence metaphysics.

A Derridean critique of hypertextuality shows this movement's commitment to the chimera of authentic communication, and hence metaphysics.

The radical appropriation of new media also purveys the democratisation of creation and invention through the radical trope of the *gift society*, about which Derrida also has something to say. It is well known that people in online communities seem prepared to develop and give away ideas, data, texts and software, without thought of immediate payment or reward. I explore this aspect of the digital economy from a design perspective elsewhere (Coyne, 2005). Suffice it to say here that the concept of the gift is of perennial interest in anthropology (Mauss, 1990), and Derrida explores the concept at length in the book *Given Time: 1. Counterfeit Money* (1992). Here Derrida explores the theme of the gift through a short story by Charles Baudelaire of an apparently simple exchange between two gentlemen and a street beggar. One gentleman gives more than the other, but the beggar is potentially the loser as the more generously valued coin is in fact counterfeit, which could get the beggar into trouble if he attempted to exchange it for food. This instance of the gift serves to amplify a series of differences. Not least are the issues of the true and the counterfeit, the just and the unjust action. For Derrida, the gift is characteristically fraught in this way, presenting various irreconcilable differences, and as such the gift also provides a model for understanding communication, language, commerce and society in general. Generosity, altruism, self-organisation without authority, grass-roots commonality of purpose and architectural activism are permeated by questions of the true and the counterfeit action.

Returning to Derrida's reflections on the archive, Derrida was aware of the speed with which communications were now possible. Electronic mail, for example, is so much faster than the postal service, but it is privileged for a more important reason.

> **electronic mail today, and even more than the fax, is on the way to transforming the entire public and private space of humanity, and first of all the limit between the private, the secret (private or public), and the public or the phenomenal.**
>
> **(Derrida and Prenowitz, 1995, p. 17)**

Lest we think that this increasing instantaneity brings people closer together, or in touch with more authentic, speech-like intercommunication, then we should recall that it has other effects that outweigh these. In a review of his essay on the archive, Lawler summarises Derrida: 'despite the increase of speed, electronic mail de-humanizes; it is still a trace, and subject to indefinite iterability. Iterability always displaces the document from any singular life (p. 99), sending it farther, to others' (Lawlor, 1998, p. 798). No matter how much contemporary literate society may value interconnectedness, access for all and the preservation of the immediacy of conversation, data is after all subject to the conditions of the archive: stored, accessed, duplicated and transmitted, a preservation that is also a destruction.

Derrida's thinking can be marshalled in critique of the democratisation of architectural practice through networked media (PEVRAV, 2008), as well as in critique of architecture's other interactions with the computer, including the claims that digital media augur a return to a more organic architecture (Lynn, 2004), that we can inhabit new realities through virtual architecture (Benedikt, 1994), and the various flavours of new digital architecture.

Architecture is similarly implicated in the problematic of the archive in so far as it is an institution for the preservation and transmission of meanings through buildings. For Derrida, architecture's investment in the archive represents both the pleasure of recollection and the will to forget. As I have referenced several times, the first step to realising the radical potential of architecture is to recognise and challenge its investment in its putative 'invariables', its institutional and institutionalised precepts: the primary importance of 'dwelling', architecture's legacies and origins, its purpose and aesthetics. Derrida notes that in architecture, the 'value of beauty, harmony and totality still reigns'. The challenge is to surrender architecture's role as 'the last fortress of metaphysics' (1986, p. 309).

So concludes this survey of Derrida for architects, and my attempt in this chapter to position Derrida within the intellectual landscape of the twentieth century. That Deconstruction in architecture as practised in the 1980s and 1990s missed the point of Derrida's contributions to intellectual life is neither a new nor an astounding insight, and is even institutionalised as critique within the movement of architectural Deconstruction itself. Derrida's thought has a life beyond the architectural movement known as Deconstruction, among the host of authors, practitioners and critics who contribute to the greater understanding of architecture and environment, and the communities and institutions that constitute and interact with architecture. As I have stressed several times, the lessons Derrida provides for architecture pertain as much to his strategies of argumentation and presentation as to the importance of his conclusions. The trope of intertextuality provides a helpful association between philosophical study and architectural design. Design is after all a process of connecting and disassembling, a richly intertextual practice.

In this book I have only touched on some of the implications of Derrida's radical and stimulating thought for architecture. There is ample scope for rigorous study of the history of Derrida's encounter with architects, the detailed analysis of how his thinking interfaces with that of other influential thinkers, how differently we might regard the profession and institution of architecture through this study, and how the many practices that make up architecture might undergo change and revision.

Notes for Further Reading

The reader who wishes to probe deeper is encouraged to look to Derrida's key ideas about language, particularly as derived from Structuralism, well explained in:

Culler, J., *On Deconstruction: Theory and Criticism after Structuralism*, London: Routledge, 1985.

Norris, C., *Deconstruction: Theory and Practice*, London: Routledge, 2002.

Hawkes, T., *Structuralism and Semiotics*, London: Routledge, 2003.

There are many excerpts and interviews with Derrida online and available through YouTube. These are from the later stages in his career. The documentary, simply entitled *Derrida*, provides the viewer with a strong sense of Derrida's personality, charisma and impact. In keeping with the medium, it is a suitable supplement to his work. The DVD includes 'outtakes' and some words from Peter Eisenman. There is scant direct reference to architecture.

Dick, K. and A. Ziering Kofman, *Derrida*, Los Angeles: Jane Doe Films Inc., 2002.

Of the works by Derrida, I would recommend the collection of essays entitled *Dissemination*. The introduction by Barbara Johnson is succinct, authoritative and revealing. The book includes Derrida's extended essay 'Plato's pharmacy', which I think best demonstrates Derrida's appeal to those with a design sensibility.

Derrida, J., *Dissemination*, trans. B. Johnson, London: Athlone, 1981.

Several key large-format books demonstrate Derrida's links with architecture:

Papadakis, A., C. Cooke and A. Benjamin (eds), *Deconstruction: Omnibus Volume*, London: Academy Editions, 1989.

Broadbent, G. and J. Glusberg (eds), *Deconstruction: A Student Guide*, London: Academy Editions, 1991.

Kipnis, J. and T. Leeser (eds), *Chora L Works: Jacques Derrida and Peter Eisenman*, New York: Monacelli Press, 1997.

Mark Wigley's book perhaps constitutes advanced reading on the theme of deconstruction in architecture, assuming a certain background understanding on the part of the reader.

Wigley, M., *The Architecture of Deconstruction: Derrida's Haunt*, Cambridge, MA: MIT Press, 1995.

References

Adorno, T.W., *The Culture Industry: Selected Essays on Mass Culture*, London: Routledge, 1991.

Alexander, C., S. Ishikawa and M. Silverstein, *A Pattern Language: Towns, Buildings, Construction*, New York: Oxford University Press, 1977.

Allen, R.E., *Greek Philosophy: Thales to Aristotle*, New York: Free Press, 1985.

Aragon, L., *Paris Peasant*, trans. S.W. Taylor, Boston: Exact Change, 1994.

Arendt, H., *The Human Condition*, Chicago, IL: University of Chicago Press, 1958.

Aristotle, *The Ethics of Aristotle: The Nicomachean Ethics*, trans. J.A.K. Thomson, London: Penguin, 1976.

Atkins, D.G. and M.L. Johnson (eds), *Writing and Reading Differently: Deconstruction and the Teaching of Composition and Literature*, Lawrence, KA: University of Kansas Press, 1985.

Augé, M., *Non-places: Introduction to an Anthropology of Supermodernity*, trans. J. Howe, London: Verso, 1995.

Augoyard, J.-F., *Step by Step: Everyday Walks in a French Urban Housing Project*, trans. D.A. Curtis, Minneapolis: University of Minnesota Press, 2007.

Augustine, *Confessions*, trans. H. Chadwick, Oxford: Oxford University Press, 1991.

Ballantyne, A., *Deleuze and Guattari for Architects*, London: Routledge, 2007.

Barthes, R., *Mythologies*, trans. A. Lavers, London: Paladin, 1973.

Benedikt, M., *Cyberspace: First Steps*, Cambridge, MA: MIT Press, 1994.

Benjamin, A., *Architectural Philosophy*, London: Athlone, 2000.

Benjamin, W., 'The work of art in the age of mechanical reproduction', in H. Arendt (ed.), *Illuminations*, London: Fontana, 1992, 1–58.

Benjamin, W., *The Arcades Project*, trans. H. Eiland and K. McLaughlin, Cambridge, MA: Harvard University Press, 2000.

Bernstein, R.J., *Beyond Objectivism and Relativism*, Oxford: Basil Blackwell, 1983.

Betti, E., 'Hermeneutics as the general methodology of the

Geisteswissenschaften', in G.L. Ormiston and A.D. Schrift (eds), *The Hermeneutic Tradition: From Ast to Ricoeur*, Albany, NY: State University of New York Press, 1990, 159–197.

Bolter, J.D., 'Topographic writing: Hypertext and the electronic writing space', in P. Delany and G.P. Landow (eds), *Hypermedia and Literary Studies*, Cambridge, MA: MIT Press, 1994, 105–118.

Breton, A., *Nadja*, trans. R. Howard, New York: Grove Press, 1960.

Breton, A., *Manifestoes of Surrealism*, Ann Arbor, MI: University of Michigan Press, 1969.

Brisson, L. and F.W. Meyerstein, *Inventing the Universe: Plato's Timaeus, the Big Bang, and the Problem of Scientific Knowledge*, Albany, NY: State University of New York Press, 1995.

Broadbent, G. and J. Glusberg (ed.), *Deconstruction: A Student Guide*, London: Academy Editions, 1991.

Caputo, J.D., *Radical Hermeneutics: Repetition, Deconstruction, and the Hermeneutical Project*, Bloomington, IN: Indiana University Press, 1987.

Colquhoun, A., *Modernity and the Classical Tradition: Architectural Essays 1980–1987*, Cambridge, MA: MIT Press, 1989.

Cooke, C., 'Russian precursors', in A. Papadakis, C. Cooke and A. Benjamin (eds), *Deconstruction: Omnibus Volume*, London: Academy Editions, 1989, 11–19.

Corbusier, L., *Towards a New Architecture*, trans. F. Etchells, New York: Dover, 1931.

Coyne, R., *Designing Information Technology in the Postmodern Age: From Method to Metaphor*, Cambridge, MA: MIT Press, 1995.

Coyne, R., *Technoromanticism: Digital Narrative, Holism, and the Romance of the Real*, Cambridge, MA: MIT Press, 1999.

Coyne, R., *Cornucopia Limited: Design and Dissent on the Internet*, Cambridge, MA: MIT Press, 2005.

Coyne, R., 'Creativity and sound: The agony of the senses', in T. Rickards, M.A. Runco and S. Moger (eds), *The Routledge Companion to Creativity*, London: Routledge, 2008, 25–36.

Culler, J., *On Deconstruction: Theory and Criticism after Structuralism*, London: Routledge, 1985.

Davis, D.A., 'Freud, Jung, and psychoanalysis', in P. Young-Eisendrath and

T. Dawson (eds), *The Cambridge Companion to Jung*, Cambridge: Cambridge University Press, 1997, 35–51.

de Certeau, M., *The Practice of Everyday Life*, trans. S. Rendall, Berkeley, CA: University of California Press, 1984.

de Zegher, C. and M. Wigley (eds), *The Activist Drawing: Retracing Situationist Architecture from Constant's New Babylon to Beyond*, Cambridge, MA: MIT Press, 2001.

Deleuze, G. and F. Guattari, *Anti-Oedipus: Capitalism and Schizophrenia*, New York: Viking Press, 1977.

Deleuze, G. and F. Guattari, *A Thousand Plateaus: Capitalism and Schizophrenia*, trans. B. Massumi, London: Athlone Press, 1988.

Derrida, J., 'Structure, sign, and play in the discourse of the human sciences', in *Writing and Difference*, London: Routledge, 1966, 278–294.

Derrida, J., 'White mythology: Metaphor in the text of philosophy', *New Literary History*, 61, 1974, 5–74.

Derrida, J., *Of Grammatology*, trans. G.C. Spivak, Baltimore, MD: Johns Hopkins University Press, 1976.

Derrida, J., *The Postcard: From Socrates to Freud and Beyond*, trans. A. Bass, Chicago, IL: Chicago University Press, 1979.

Derrida, J., 'Plato's pharmacy', in *Dissemination*, trans. B. Johnson, London: Athlone, 1981, 61–171.

Derrida, J., 'Différance', in *Margins of Philosophy*, Chicago, IL: University of Chicago Press, 1982a, 3–27.

Derrida, J., 'Signature event context', in *Margins of Philosophy*, Chicago, IL: University of Chicago Press, 1982b, 307–330.

Derrida, J., 'Tympanum', in *Margins of Philosophy*, Chicago, IL: University of Chicago Press, 1982c, ix–xxix.

Derrida, J., 'The principle of reason: The university in the eyes of its pupils', *Diacritics*, 13, 1983, 3–20.

Derrida, J., 'Point de Folie: Maintenant l'architecture', in N. Leach (ed.), *Rethinking Architecture: A Reader in Cultural Theory*, London: Routledge, 1986, 305–317.

Derrida, J., *Edmund Husserl's 'Origin of Geometry': An Introduction*, trans. J.P. Leavey, Lincoln, NE: University of Nebraska Press, 1989a.

Derrida, J., 'Jacques Derrida in discussion with Christopher Norris', in
A. Papadakis, C. Cooke and A. Benjamin (eds), *Deconstruction: Omnibus
Volume*, London: Academy Editions, 1989b, 71–78.

Derrida, J., *Given Time: 1. Counterfeit Money*, trans. P. Kamuf, Chicago, IL:
University of Chicago Press, 1992.

Derrida, J., *Aporias*, trans. T. Dutoit, Stanford, CA: Stanford University Press,
1993.

Derrida, J., 'Chora', in J. Kipnis and T. Leeser (eds), *Chora L Works*, New York:
Monacelli Press, 1997, 15–32.

Derrida, J. and H.P. Hanel, 'A letter to Peter Eisenman', *Assemblage*, 12, 1990,
6–13.

Derrida, J. and E. Prenowitz, 'Archive fever: A Freudian impression', *Diacritics*,
25: 2, 1995, 9–63.

Descartes, R., *Discourse on Method and the Meditations*, trans. F.E. Sutcliffe,
Harmondsworth: Penguin, 1968.

Dick, K. and A. Ziering Kofman, *Derrida*, Los Angeles: Jane Doe Films Inc, 2002.

Donougho, M., 'The language of architecture', *Journal of Aesthetic Education*,
21: 3, 1987, 53–67.

Durand, J.-N.-L., *Précis of the Lectures on Architecture*, trans. D. Britt, Los
Angeles, CA: Getty Research Institute, 2000.

Eisenman, P., 'Post/El cards: A reply to Jacques Derrida', *Assemblage*, 12, 1990,
14–17.

Eliade, M., *The Two and the One*, trans. J.M. Cohen, London: Harvill Press, 1965.

Esslin, M., *The Theatre of the Absurd*, London: Eyre and Spottiswood, 1961.

Evans, R., 'Towards anarchitecture', *Architectural Association Quarterly*, 2: 1,
1970, 58 and 69.

Feenberg, A., *Transforming Technology: A Critical Theory Revisited*, Oxford:
Oxford University Press, 2002.

Foucault, M., 'Of other spaces', *Diacritics*, 16: 1, 1986, 22–27.

Freud, S., 'The "uncanny" ', in A. Dickson (ed.), *The Penguin Freud Library,
Volume 14: Art and Literature*, Harmondsworth: Penguin, 1990, 335–376.

Freud, S., 'Three essays on the theory of sexuality', in A. Richards (ed.), *The
Penguin Freud Library, Volume 7: On Sexuality*, Harmondsworth: Penguin,
1991, 31–169.

Gadamer, H.-G., *Truth and Method*, trans. J. Weinsheimer, New York: Seabury Press, 1975.

Gallagher, S., *Hermeneutics and Education*, Albany, NY: State University of New York Press, 1992.

Giddens, A., *The Constitution of Society: Outline of the Theory of Structuration*, Cambridge: Polity, 1984.

Glendinning, M., *Architecture's Evil Empire? The Triumph and Tragedy of Global Modernism*, London: Reaktion, 2010.

Harris, R., *Foundations of Indo-European Comparative Philology 1800–1850 Volume 1*, Chippenham: Routledge, 1999.

Havelock, E.A., *The Muse Learns to Write: Reflections on Orality and Literacy from Antiquity to the Present*, New Haven, CT: Yale University Press, 1986.

Hawkes, T., *Structuralism and Semiotics*, London: Methuen, 1977.

Heidegger, M., *Being and Time*, trans. J. Macquarrie and E. Robinson, London: SCM Press, 1962.

Heidegger, M., 'Building, dwelling, thinking', in *Poetry, Language, Thought*, New York: Harper & Row, 1971, 143–161.

Heisenberg, W., *Physics and Philosophy: The Revolution in Modern Science*, New York: Harper & Row, 1958.

Hill, J., *Actions of Architecture: Architects and Creative Users*, London: Routledge, 2003.

Holmes, B., 'Do-it-yourself geopolitics: Map of the world upside down', in PEVRAV (ed.), *Urban Act: A Handbook of Alternative Practice*, Paris: European Platform for Alternative Practice and Research on the City, Atelier d'Architecture Autogérée, 2008, 300–306.

Huizinga, J., *Homo Ludens: A Study of the Play Element in Culture*, Boston, MA: Beacon Press, 1955.

Hyde, L., *Trickster Makes This World: Mischief, Myth and Art*, New York: North Point Press, 1998.

Jakobson, R. and M. Halle, *Fundamentals of Language*, The Hague: Mouton, 1956.

Jameson, F., *The Prison-House of Language: A Critical Account of Structuralism and Russian Formalism*, Princeton, NJ: Princeton University Press, 1972.

Jameson, F., *Archaeologies of the Future: The Desire Called Utopia and Other Science Fiction*, London: Verso, 2005.

Jencks, C., 'Deconstruction: The pleasure of absence', in A. Papadakis, C. Cooke and A. Benjamin (eds), *Deconstruction: Omnibus Volume*, London: Academy Editions, 1989, 119–131.

Jencks, C. and G. Baird (eds), *Meaning in Architecture*, London: Barrie & Rockliff, 1969.

Johnson, B., 'Translator's introduction', in J. Derrida, *Dissemination*, London: Athlone, 1981, vii–xxxiii.

Johnson, B., 'Teaching deconstructively', in G.D. Atkins and M.L. Johnson (eds), *Writing and Reading Differently: Deconstruction and the Teaching of Composition and Literature*, Lawrence, KA: University Press of Kansas, 1985, 140–148.

Kant, I. and P. Guyer, *Critique of the Power of Judgment*, Cambridge: Cambridge University Press, 2000.

Kipnis, J., 'Twisting the separatrix', *Assemblage*, 14, 1991, 30–61.

Kipnis, J. and T. Leeser (eds), *Chora L Works: Jacques Derrida and Peter Eisenman*, New York: Monacelli Press, 1997.

Klein, N., *No Logo*, London: Harper Perennial, 2005.

Koolhaas, R., 'Junk space', in R. Koolhaas, AMO and OMA (eds), *Content*, Cologne: Taschen, 2004, 162–171.

Kropotkin, P.A. and M. Shatz, *The Conquest of Bread and Other Writings*, Cambridge; New York: Cambridge University Press, 1995.

Lacan, J., *The Four Fundamental Concepts of Psychoanalysis*, trans. A. Sheridan, London: Penguin, 1979.

Lamont, M., 'How to become a dominant French philosopher: The case of Jacques Derrida', *American Journal of Sociology*, 93: 3, 1987, 584–622.

Landow, G.P., 'Hypertext as collage-writing', in P. Delany and G.P. Landow (eds), *Hypermedia and Literary Studies*, Cambridge, MA: MIT Press, 1994, 150–170.

Landow, G.P. and P. Delany, 'Hypertext, hypermedia and literary studies: The state of the art', in P. Delany and G.P. Landow (eds), *Hypermedia and Literary Studies*, Cambridge, MA: MIT Press, 1994, 3–50.

Laugier, M.-A., *An Essay on Architecture*, trans. W. Herrmann and A. Herrmann, Los Angeles, CA: Hennessey and Ingalls, 1977.

Lawlor, L., 'Review: Memory becomes electra', *Review of Politics*, 60: 4, 1998, 796–798.

Lévi-Strauss, C., *Structural Anthropology 1*, London: Penguin, 1963.

Lynn, G. (ed.), *Folding in Architecture* (rev. edn), Chichester: Wiley-Academy, 2004.

Lyotard, J.-F., *The Postmodern Condition: A Report on Knowledge*, Manchester: Manchester University Press, 1986.

McEwen, I., *Vitruvius: Writing the Body of Architecture*, Cambridge, MA: MIT Press, 2003.

McLuhan, M., *The Gutenberg Galaxy: The Making of Typographic Man*, Toronto: University of Toronto Press, 1962.

McMahon, A., *Understanding Language Change*, Cambridge: Cambridge University Press, 1994.

Marcuse, H., *One-Dimensional Man: Studies in the Ideology of Advanced Industrial Society*, London: Routledge, 1991.

Martin, L., 'Transpositions: On the intellectual origins of Tschumi's architectural theory', *Assemblage*, 11, 1990, 22–35.

Marx, K., 'The Poverty of Philosophy', in D. McClellan (ed.), *Karl Marx: Selected Writings*, Oxford: Oxford University Press, 1977, 195–215.

Mauss, M., *The Gift: The Form and Reason for Exchange in Archaic Societies*, trans. W.D. Halls, New York: W.W. Norton, 1990.

Meadows, D.H., N.L. Meadows, J. Randers and W.W. Behrens, *The Limits of Growth, a Report for the Club of Rome's Project on the Predicament of Mankind*, London: Potomac, 1972.

Michelfelder, D.P. and R.E. Palmer (eds), *Dialogue and Deconstruction: The Gadamer–Derrida Encounter*, Albany, NY: State University of New York Press, 1989.

Mikics, D., *Who Was Jacques Derrida? An Intellectual Biography*, London: Yale University Press, 2010.

Mill, J.S., *On Liberty*, London: Routledge, 1991.

Motycka Weston, D., 'Communicating vessels: André Breton and his atelier, home and personal museum in Paris', *Architectural Theory Review*, 11: 2, 2006, 101–128.

Norris, C., *Deconstruction: Theory and Practice*, London: Routledge, 1982.

Ong, W.J., *Orality and Literacy: The Technologizing of the Word*, London: Routledge, 2002.

Papadakis, A., C. Cooke and A. Benjamin (eds), *Deconstruction: Omnibus Volume*, London: Academy Editions, 1989.

Papanek, V., *Design for the Real World: Human Ecology and Social Change*, New York: Pantheon, 1971.

Patin, T., 'From deep structure to an architecture in suspense: Peter Eisenman, Structuralism, and Deconstruction', *Journal of Architectural Education*, 47: 2, 1993, 88–100.

Pérez-Gómez, A., 'Chora: The space of architectural representation', in A. Pérez-Gómez and S. Parcell (eds), *Chora 1: Intervals in the Philosophy of Architecture*, Montreal: McGill-Queen's University Press, 1994, 1–34.

PEVRAV, *Urban Act: A Handbook of Alternative Practice*, Paris: European Platform for Alternative Practice and Research on the City, Atelier d'Architecture Autogérée, 2008.

Piaget, J., *Structuralism*, trans. C. Maschler, New York: Basic Books, 1970.

Plato, *The Timaeus of Plato*, trans. R.D. Archer-Hind, London: Macmillan, 1888.

Plato, *The Republic of Plato*, trans. F.M. Cornford, London: Oxford University Press, 1941.

Plato, *Timaeus and Critias*, trans. D. Lee, London: Penguin, 1965.

Plato, *Phaedrus*, trans. R. Waterfield, Oxford: Oxford University Press, 2002.

Popper, K.R., *The Poverty of Historicism*, London: Routledge & Kegan Paul, 1957.

Powell, J., *Jacques Derrida: A Biography*, London: Continuum, 2006.

Rafael, V., 'The cell phone and the crowd: Messianic politics in the contemporary Philippines', in W.H.K. Chun and T. Keenan (eds), *New Media Old Media*, London: Routledge, 2006, 297–314.

Rand, A., *The Fountainhead*, London: Grafton, 1972.

Rawes, P., *Irigaray for Architects*, London: Routledge, 2007.

Rendell, J., *Art and Architecture: A Place Between*, London: I.B. Tauris, 2006.

Rheingold, H., *The Virtual Community: Homesteading on the Electronic Frontier*, Reading, MA: Addison Wesley, 1993.

Richards, K.M., *Derrida Reframed: A Guide for the Arts Student*, London: I.B. Tauris, 2008.

Ricoeur, P., *Freud and Philosophy: An Essay in Interpretation*, trans. D. Savage, New Haven, CT: Yale University Press, 1970.

Rorty, R., *Contingency, Irony, and Solidarity*, Cambridge: Cambridge University Press, 1989.

Rorty, R., 'Remarks on deconstruction and pragmatism', in C. Mouffe (ed.), *Deconstruction and Pragmatism*, London: Routledge, 1996a, 13–18.

Rorty, R., 'Response to Ernesto Laclau', in C. Mouffe (ed.), *Deconstruction and Pragmatism*, London: Routledge, 1996b, 69–76.

Rousseau, J.-J., *Essay on the Origin of Language*, trans. J.H. Moran and A. Gode, Chicago, IL: University of Chicago Press, 1966.

Rousseau, J.-J., *Confessions*, trans. A. Scholar, Oxford: Oxford University Press, 2008.

Runes, D.D., *Dictionary of Philosophy*, New York: Philosophical Library, 1942.

Ruskin, J., *The Seven Lamps of Architecture*, London: Everyman's Library, 1956.

Rykwert, J., *On Adam's House in Paradise: The Idea of the Primitive Hut in Architectural History*, Cambridge, MA: MIT Press, 1997.

Sallis, J., *Chorology: On Beginnings in Plato's* Timaeus, Bloomington, IN: Indiana University Press, 1999.

Saussure, F. de, *Course in General Linguistics*, trans. R. Harris, London: Duckworth, 1983.

Scholem, G.G., *Major Trends in Jewish Mysticism*, London: Thames & Hudson, 1955.

Scruton, R., *The Aesthetics of Architecture*, Princeton, NJ: Princeton University Press, 1979.

Seligmann, K. and C. Seligmann, 'Architecture and language: Notes on a metaphor', *Journal of Architectural Education*, 30: 4, 1977, 23–27.

Sellars, J., 'The point of view of the cosmos: Deleuze, romanticism, stoicism', *Pli (The Warwick Journal of Philosophy)*, 8, 1999, 1–24.

Sharr, A., *Heidegger's Hut*, Cambridge, MA: MIT Press, 2006.

Sharr, A., *Heidegger for Architects*, London: Routledge, 2007.

Shaw, R., *The Activist's Handbook: A Primer*, Berkeley, CA: University of California Press, 2001.

Smith, A., *The Theory of Moral Sentiments*, Indianapolis: Liberty Fund, 1984.

Snodgrass, A.B., *Architecture, Time and Eternity: Studies in the Stellar and Temporal Symbolism of Traditional Buildings, Volume 2*, New Delhi: Aditya Prakashan, 1990.

Snodgrass, A. and R. Coyne, *Interpretation in Architecture: Design as a Way of Thinking*, London: Routledge, 2006.

Sokal, A.D. and J. Bricmont, *Intellectual Impostures: Postmodern Philosophers' Abuse of Science*, London: Profile Books, 2003.

Soltan, M., 'Architecture as a kind of writing', *American Literary History*, 3: 2, 1991, 405–419.

Summerson, J., *The Classical Language of Architecture*, Cambridge, MA: MIT Press, 1963.

Tafuri, M., *Architecture and Utopia: Design and Capitalist Development*, trans. B.L. La Penta, Cambridge, MA: MIT Press, 1996.

Taylor, A.E., *A Commentary on Plato's* Timaeus, London: Oxford University Press, 1928.

Tschumi, B., *Architecture and Disjunction*, Cambridge, MA: MIT Press, 1994.

Tschumi, B., 'Introduction', in J. Kipnis and T. Leeser (eds), *Chora L Works*, New York: Monacelli Press, 1997, 125.

Turner, V., *The Forest of Symbols: Aspects of Ndembu Ritual*, Ithaca, NY: Cornell University Press, 1967.

Ulmer, G.L., 'Textshop for post(e)pedagogy', in G.D. Atkins and M.L. Johnson (eds), *Writing and Reading Differently: Deconstruction and the Teaching of Composition and Literature*, Lawrence, KA: University Press of Kansas, 1985, 38–64.

Urry, J., *The Tourist Gaze: Leisure and Travel in Contemporary Societies*, London: Sage, 1990.

Venturi, R., D. Scott Brown and S. Izenour, *Learning from Las Vegas: The Forgotten Symbolism of Architectural Form*, Cambridge, MA: MIT Press, 1993.

Vidler, A., *The Architectural Uncanny: Essays in the Modern Unhomely*, Cambridge, MA: MIT Press, 1995.

Vitruvius, P., *Vitruvius: The Ten Books on Architecture*, trans. M.H. Morgan, New York: Dover Publications, 1960.

Watkin, D., *Morality and Architecture: The Development of a Theme in Architectural History and Theory in the Gothic Revival to the Modern Movement*, Oxford: Clarendon Press, 1977.

Wigley, M., 'Postmortem architecture: The taste of Derrida', *Perspectiva*, 23, 1987, 156–172.

Wigley, M., *The Architecture of Deconstruction: Derrida's Haunt*, Cambridge, MA: MIT Press, 1995.

Wittgenstein, L., *Philosophical Investigations*, trans. G.E.M. Anscombe, Oxford: Blackwell, 1953.

Zavarzadeh, M. and D. Morton, 'Theory pedagogy politics: The crisis of the subject in the humanities', *Boundary*, 2: 15, 1986–1987, 1–22.

Žižek, S., *The Sublime Object of Ideology*, London: Verso, 1989.

Index

activism 86–7
Adorno, Theodor 77
advertising 89
agonistics 5
Alexander, Christopher xvi, 9
architecture 2, 6, 8–10, 17–18, 33–4;
    as the last fortress of metaphysics
    xvii, 60, 97
archive 74, 83
Aristotle 63, 71, 95
Art 34, 68, 77, 79, 80–1
Augé, Marc 72
Augoyard, Jean-François 58–9

Barthes, Roland 15, 20, 22–3, 36, 43
Being xx–xxii, 79
Breton, André xxiv, 2, 58
Broadbent, Geoffrey 37, 39, 100

Caputo, John xviii, 6, 78, 81–2, 86
chaos 72
chora xxii, 38, 45, 48–55, 64–73
Chora L Works 36, 45–7, 57–9, 66,
    100
Ciph 85
communication 31–3
community 26, 29, 79–82, 85;
    interpretive 80; linguistic 14, 17
confounding oppositions 7

conservatism 76
Constructivism 2
Coop Himmelblau 82
correspondence 13
Counterfeit 95
Culler, Jonathan 8, 39, 99
cyberspace 61

de Certeau 59, 90
Deconstruction 39, 56, 59–60, 93;
    and literature 92; criticism of 47,
    97; defined 10; named xiv
deep structure 19
Deleuze, Giles 63, 72, 83, 86, 90
Derrida, Jacques; in Algeria xiv; and
    architecture 2, 24, 36–60;
    biography xiv; career xiv, 75, 77;
    diffusion of ideas 36; documentary
    of 82, 99; education xiv; and
    Eisenman 39–59; in Paris xiv, 36,
    49, 51, 77; reception of 7, 36,
    77–8; style of writing xv, xix–xxiv; in
    the USA xiv, 36, 45, 53, 85
Descartes, Rene 80
design 10, 97
différance xx–xxii, 47
difference xxi–xxii, 16–21, 31–3
disjunction 37–8, 72
documentary 82, 99

drawing 32, 34, 45, 51

École Normale Supérieure xiv
education 91
Eisenman, Peter 2, 36–59, 66–7, 87, 92
everyday 58–9, 90

fashion 20
formalism 39
forms xvi, 64–6, 70
Foucault, Michel xxii, 72, 90
foundations xvi–xvii
Frankfurt School 37, 76
Freud, Sigmund xxiv, 49, 68, 72, 83
Fuller, Buckminster 37

Gadamer, Hans-Georg 77, 79–80, 82
Gallagher, Shaun 77, 79–80, 93
Gehry, Frank 39–40, 52
Giddens, Anthony 22
grammatology 31, 36

Hadid, Zaha 45
Hawkes, Terrence 8, 21–2, 99
Heidegger, Martin xxi, 8, 37–8, 79, 85
Heisenberg, Werner xviii
Hermes 70
Hestia 70
heterotopias 72–3
Huizinga, Johan 4
hypertext 93–4
hypodoche 65, 68

idealism 61

institutions 74, 83, 86
Intelligible 30, 49, 62–6, 71
Internet 38, 90, 93–4
interpretation 78–9
intertextuality 25, 29–31, 33, 57–8; and design 97; and hypertext 94–5
irony xxii

Jameson, Fredric 8, 13–15, 19, 28, 64
Jencks, Charles 8, 37, 47
Johnson, Barbara xx, 92, 94, 99
juxtapositions and oppositions 2

Kafka, Franz 43
Kant, Immanuel 38, 67, 68
khora 67
Kipnis, Jeffrey 36, 43, 45, 47–57, 100
Koolhaas, Rem 6

Lacan, Jacques xxii, 15, 72, 83
Landow, George 93, 95
Language; and architecture 8–24; and history 11–13
Laugier, Marc-Antoine 12, 13
Le Corbusier 6, 61
Lefebvre, Henri 90
Lévi-Strauss, Claude 20–2, 36
Libeskind, Daniel 39
Lyotard, Jean-François 43, 68

McLuhan, Marshall 26
Marxism 76
Mauss, Marcel 95

meaning 8, 23–4, 37; and metaphysics 23
metaphor 25, 31
metaphysics xvi–xxi, 23–4, 53, 60, 75
Mikics, David xiv, xix, 36, 52, 77
mirror 68

Nietzsche, Friedrich Wilhelm 52
nonsense 72
Norris, Christopher 8, 99

opposition 7, 18, 22, 31, 38
origin xix, 11
other spaces 61–2, 64, 72

palimpsest 49
Palladio, Andrea xvi, 10, 29
Parc de la Villette 36, 42–4, 47, 50, 58–60
Pérez-Gómez, Alberto 69–70
PEVRAV 88, 90–1, 96
Phaedrus 25, 27–8, 30, 33, 94
pharmakeus 29
pharmakon 30
Phenomenology xxi, 8, 77–9
philology 11
philosophy xvii, 1, 34, 53, 75
Piaget, Jean 16
Plato 25–34, 48–51, 61–71, 94–5
Platonism 25, 63
postcard 23
Postmodernism 37, 42–3
Poststructuralism 10, 22, 34
practice 8, 59, 74, 90, 99

Pragmatism 1, 7, 63, 73, 78
prejudice 80
proto-writing 31–3
pun 52

radical hermeneutics 81
radical media 93
radical pedagogy 91
readymades xxiii, xxiv
rhetoric 25
RIBA 81
Ricoeur, Paul 82
Romanticism 37
Rorty, Richard 1, 7, 73
Rousseau, Jean-Jacques 11, 27–8, 75, 78
Rykwert, Joseph 12

Saussure, Ferdinand de 11–14, 16–19, 28, 32
scapegoat 29, 94
semiotics 8, 99
Sensible 48–9, 62–4, 66, 71
Serres, Michel 83
sign systems and difference 16
signature xxii
Situationism 2
Snodgrass, Adrian 22, 79
Socrates 25, 27, 30
space; and chora 38, 45, 48–9; other 61–73; and paradox 71
spatiality 73
speech 27, 33
Stoicism 63–4
surprise 24, 82

Surrealism xxiii, 2, 72, 82
syntax 10, 41

Tafuri, Manfredo 37, 77
Theuth 27
Thinking 1
Timaeus 48–51, 61, 64–5, 67, 69
Tschumi, Bernard 3, 37, 42–5, 59–60,
    82; disagreement with Eisenman
    50–1
Twitter 26
tympanum xxiv

universities xiv, 85, 91

Venturi, Robert 37, 39
Vidler, Anthony 72
Vitruvius, Pollio xxiv, 12, 63

walking 49, 58–9
Wigley, Mark 36, 38, 90, 100
writing xv, 25–8, 30–4; as a drug 28;
    origins of 25, 27

Žižek, Slovoj 72